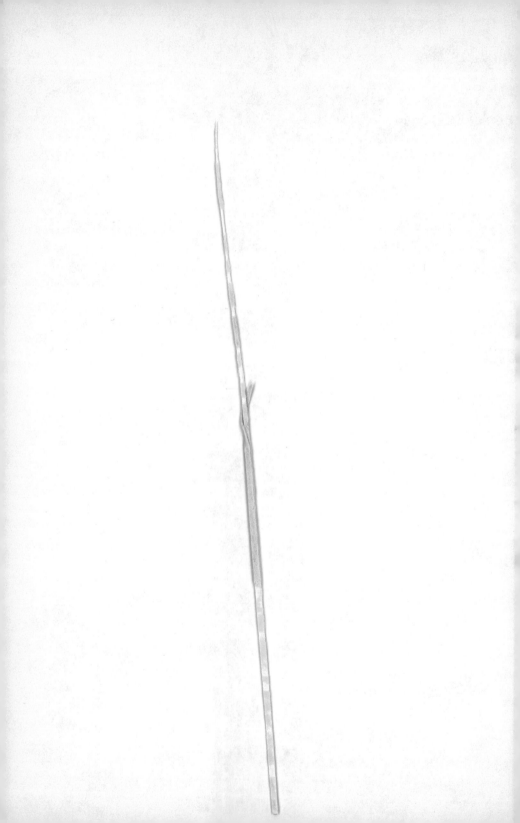

Systems Contracting

Systems Contracting

A NEW PURCHASING TECHNIQUE

BY RALPH A. BOLTON

AMERICAN MANAGEMENT ASSOCIATION, INC.

The softbound edition of this book has been distributed without charge to AMA members enrolled in the Manufacturing and Purchasing Divisions. Those members who are enrolled in other divisions, or who wish extra copies, may order the book in a hardbound edition at $4.50 per copy. Price to nonmembers, $6.75.

The term "Systems Contracting" is registered by The Carborundum Company.

Library of Congress catalog card number: 66-30189.

About the Author

Ralph A. Bolton is systems purchasing coordinator for The Carborundum Company in Niagara Falls, New York. He received a B.S. degree from the University of Buffalo.

Mr. Bolton was formerly assistant to director of purchases of The Carborundum Company, Niagara Falls, New York. In this capacity he was responsible for the development of a new purchasing concept called Systems Contracts. As a result of this activity, The Carborundum Company greatly reduced procurement costs and improved service between the plant and the vendor.

For the past two years Mr. Bolton has assisted corporations throughout the United States in developing similar techniques based on the Systems Contract concept.

In addition Mr. Bolton has been a frequent lecturer at the American Management Association in New York and has authored several articles for national trade publications.

Foreword

The materials acquisition-retention cycle in the overall purchasing process is undergoing rapid changes. Fortunately there are dedicated men continually creating improved techniques as well as a body of literature reporting these innovations. At the 1963 N.A.P.A. Convention in Dallas, Texas, one of the guest speakers was hopeful that the best materials system would yet be invented, the best purchasing techniques created, the best negotiating strategies planned, and the best purchasing men developed. I subscribed then to this enthusiasm for a better future in purchasing and feel Systems Contracting is a stepping-stone to it.

The reader may be already familiar with the general concept of Systems Contracting and be seeking in this book more specific details of it. I submit that he will get that and more. Systems Contracting, as presented here by the author, represents change, challenge, and opportunity. It represents change in thinking more critically about the primary responsibilities of the purchasing function—that is, sourcing and prices paid. Systems Contracting means more deliberate sourcing and elaborate contracting. It challenges the whole acquisition-retention cycle and the need for questionable controls. It suggests where to place real controls (not, perhaps, in any particular department but in the contract with the supplier). If we are willing and able to change and to accept the challenge, then the opportunity is wide open through Systems Contracting to a better life for present-day purchasing people and their suppliers.

In a large, diversified corporation such as Brunswick, one of the challenging tasks of purchasing management is to create common denominators among purchasing locations, and Systems Contracting is of vital interest to us and all locations because it can be appropriately implemented regardless of plant size.

This work is a well-timed response to the tremendous interest and inquiry received by the American Management Association for information about Systems Contracting. The American Management Association is to be congratulated for publishing this book dedicated, as is AMA, to the education of management by management.

In our enthusiasm for the concept of Systems Contracting, we are grateful to the author for helping to show the way to the future.

Michael J. Loftus
Corporate Purchasing Manager
Brunswick Corporation
Chicago, Illinois

Contents

Introduction

Systems Contracting or Systems Contracts is one of the most widely discussed yet least understood concepts to invade American industry during the past decade. Essentially a purchasing concept, Systems Contracting results in an agreement between buyer and seller which is then called a Systems Contract. It is of vital interest in virtually every phase of the business cycle because of the overall effect on plant efficiency and corporate profit. Management is aware of the potential savings that an efficient procurement operation can produce. Systems Contracts is one method that has proved successful in securing that efficiency.

Systems Contracts has been compared to blanket-order buying, national agreements, automatic purchasing, and, it seems, just about every new purchasing idea that has come along; yet each of these methods is but a part of the total concept. Perhaps the main reason for this confusion or lack of understanding is that a Systems Contract is basically a very simple procedure. All too often management seems to think that a sophisticated scheme involving endless controls and perhaps automated equipment is essential for effectiveness, when in reality all that is needed is common sense. This is not to say, however, that we have abandoned internal controls. On the contrary, the controls associated with Systems Contracts have proved far more effective than those normally associated with standard purchasing practices.

The term Systems Contracts is derived from the fact that it is a simplified *system* that describes a method of procurement which is affirmed by a *contractual* understanding. A Systems Contract is a total corporate technique designed to assist the buyer and seller to improve the reordering of repetitive-use materials or services with an absolute minimum of administrative expense and with the maintenance of adequate business controls. The objective of Systems Contracts is to simplify reordering procedures and contribute to corporate profits. Again, these objectives refer to buyer and seller alike.

It must be emphasized that it is the end cost or value of the buy that is important, and not just the price paid. Very often the price paid for materials or services covered by a Systems Contract is higher than in some other system, but the end cost will always be lower.

The term administrative expense used in the definition includes *all* areas involved in the procurement cycle: manufacturing, stores, accounting, purchasing, receiving, and supplier functions. The reduction of administrative expense must be an overall reduction and not merely a shuffling of duties from one department to another. The simplification of the order procedure through the application of the Systems Contract will result in improved delivery of materials.

The term Systems Contracts was first used in 1962 by The Carborundum Company to identify this revolutionary buying technique. The method of procurement used by Carborundum prior to Systems Contracts was very similar to that employed by many corporations that employ a purchase order technique. The Carborundum Company is a multiplant corporation with headquarters in Niagara Falls, New York. Each plant location operates under a broad corporate policy and is regarded as a profit center. Some plant facilities employ several thousand workers, while others represent small operations which involve less than a hundred people. Some manufacturing operations are on a production-line basis while others are strictly job shops. Product mix varies from abrasives to heavy production machinery. It should be noted that, even with all of these variables, Systems Contracts has consistently proved to be an acceptable means of procurement at Carborundum. In fact, as the concept was expanded to include additional product categories throughout the corporation, it began to make a direct and favorable impact on the profits of the company. During the past several years companies in the chemical, optical, electrical, basic metal, and other industries have adopted Systems Contracts with similar results. Systems Contracts has now matured into a recognized method of procurement.

Most large corporations adhere to high principles in business management and are proud of their ethical standing in the business world. Systems Contracts is based on that priceless ingredient, "business integrity." This is true not only of the buying company but also of the selling organization. It must be the intention of all parties to operate along strictly ethical lines for Systems Contracts to prove effective.

In general, we will proceed as follows in this book: first, we will try to gain an understanding of the traditional procurement method and compare it with Systems Contracts; second, we will describe in detail how to set up a working program of Systems Contracts.

CHAPTER I

Evaluating the Traditional Purchase Order Method

The first step in evaluating an existing system is to consider the stated policies of the company where they exist. Usually these are published in a corporate policy or procedures manual. Depending on the size of the company and the scope of its operation, these policies may be relatively simple or quite complex.

The headquarters of a multidivisional or multiplant corporation such as Carborundum usually establishes the basic policy, and the various divisions and operating plants stipulate a variety of procedures, based on that overall corporate policy, to meet the needs of the local operation.

Most corporate manuals are broad enough to permit the application of Systems Contracts procedures. Where the policy prohibits such a program, the overall benefits of the Systems Contract concept will in all probability warrant revision (the case at Carborundum).

The purchasing manual is of prime importance and, as such, should be given first consideration; other departmental procedures such as those for accounting should also be considered.

A purchasing policy statement usually includes the following basic objectives:

1. To protect the best interests of the company.
2. To develop adequate and trained personnel.

17

3. To purchase materials of the right quality, in the right quantities, from the right source, at the right time, at the right price.

4. To promote fair and friendly relations with all concerned.

In addition, the ethical standards of the corporation usually find expression in statements to the effect that purchasing must employ competitive procedures based on bids of standard specifications rather than branded names and on the maintenance of strict confidence concerning the nature of competitive quotes.

Unfortunately, although most policy statements of corporations are well meaning, their actual application in a line operation is difficult because of the nature of the functions performed and the personnel involved. Much of the cause of purchasing inefficiency, compared with other areas of management, is due to obsolete procedures. Systems Contracts will bring into focus the value of having a flexible policy, capable of taking advantage of new techniques, rather than having a rigid code.

Perhaps normal terminology is the largest stumbling block to understanding Systems Contracts. Essentially, purchasing is a management function while buying is a clerical operation. Admittedly, many purchasing policies, as indicated above, refer to a buying function; however, this does not necessarily mean that the policy is correct. In evaluating the existing procurement method, complete objectivity must be maintained.

THE STANDARD PURCHASE ORDER PROCEDURE

The use of an actual case study may serve to illuminate the problems and principles involved in evaluating the traditional procurement method. We will concentrate on a repetitive-use material which represents one of the most familiar problems confronting purchasing today. By understanding present purchasing problems, the advantages of Systems Contracts will become apparent.

The circumstances of this case are as follows:

1. Work area involved: general office.

2. Material required: stationery.

3. Specification: wooden lead pencil, No. 2 standard.

4. Point of need: clerical personnel.
5. Procedure: clerk determines need for a replacement pencil and issued materials requisition.

Admittedly this seems absurdly simple, but this type of transaction is repeated over and over every day in every company. The repetitiveness of this type of transaction is the basis for establishing Systems Contracts. An objective appraisal of the requisition for a pencil as outlined can point up the distinction between buying and purchasing. A flow chart of the standard purchase order procedure is illustrated in Exhibit 1.

As soon as the employee determined a need for a replacement pencil, many of the objectives of purchasing were already secured:

1. The right material: a black lead pencil.
2. The right quality: No. 2 standard.
3. The right quantity: one (usually one box).
4. The right place: the office work area.
5. The right time: now.

The employee probably determined the price structure by requesting the same specifications as previously used. The main function of the purchasing department in this transaction was to:

1. Determine the vendor.
2. Figure the economic order quantity (EOQ).
3. Negotiate to the actual purchase price.
4. Determine delivery date.

This was the procedure followed for one lead pencil, but for how many other items would this same analysis apply? The answer is virtually every repetitive-use material required in the conduct of normal business operations. Many companies use upward of 30,000 individual items which could be classed as repetitive. This fact is responsible for one of the most important conclusions concerning the purchasing function: *80 percent of all purchasing activity involves repetitive-use materials and represents 20 percent of the dollars committed.*

This means just what it says. Most purchasing departments spend a disproportionate amount of their time (80 percent) buying low-value (20 percent of dollars spent) repetitive supplies. It is not uncommon to find maintenance, repair, and operating supply (MRO) buyers in many companies whose sole responsibility is to handle this portion of the purchase orders issued. Invariably these people are swamped with

Flow Chart of Standard Purchase Order Procedure

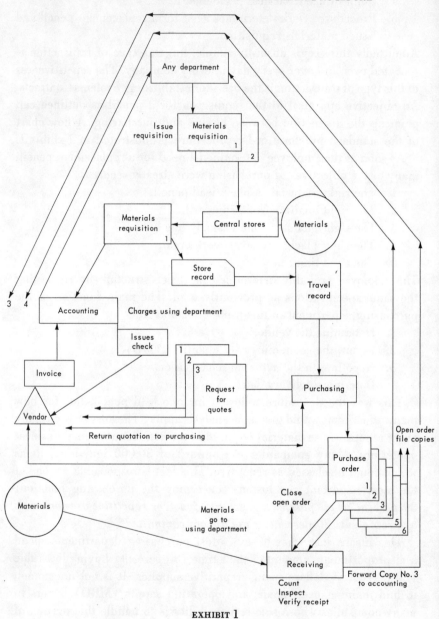

EXHIBIT 1

work and are always looking for some way of conserving time in order to improve the service to the plant.

Once the need for pencils was established, the supply of pencils was replenished from a point of availability commonly referred to as a stationery storeroom. This is a company-controlled inventory which consists of repetitive-use materials and is designed to provide fast, efficient service to the using areas. The storekeeper is usually responsible for maintaining the inventory levels and, as such, concentrates on those items which show maximum usage. Two control mechanisms force the storekeeper to concentrate on the high-use items: (1) physical space available because the storeroom is limited; and (2) amount of dollars available for investment because this is restricted.

Many of these low-value stores items do not affect the overall productive capacity of a company in any significant manner. Items such as paper towels, hand soap, floor cleaners, wiping rags, and so on take up a considerable amount of storage area, yet are relatively low in value and importance when compared to a replacement part for a piece of productive equipment. Replacement parts are rarely stocked in any quantity because of low turnover; consequently, when a need arises for such material, purchasing must come to the rescue. A basic conclusion regarding company storerooms is: *90 percent of stores transactions are for low-value repetitive materials affecting nonproductive plant needs.*

Most companies employ a simple internal ordering process to facilitate acquisition of stores materials by authorized personnel. In reality, the one in need buys and pays for his materials through the use of a material requisition, an example of which is shown in Exhibit 2.

This form is usually a two- or three-part document which is completed by hand by the requisitioner and is approved by a superior. The requisitioner may be an hourly employee; but the approval point, which is part of the control, is probably a salaried employee of supervisory capacity. The accounting control of this type of requirement is accomplished through the use of a departmental job or employee charge number. The value of the material ordered on the requisition is charged to the department represented by the charge number, and credit is given to the stores inventory.

In practice, this system works quite well, but a realistic control of this type of transaction is difficult to manage, especially with respect to

MATERIALS REQUISITION—TRADITIONAL METHOD

CARBORUNDUM
MATERIAL REQUISITION

REQUISITION NO. 1

C H A R G E T O	ACCOUNT NO. 1 2 3 4
	DETAIL NO.
	SHOP ORDER NO.
	E. A. NO.

TO: Office Supplies

Quantity and Unit Ordered	Catalog or Material #	DESCRIPTION	Vendor or Inventory #	Quantity Issued	Std. Price Per Unit	Actual Price Per Unit	Extended Value
4 doz.		Black Lead #2 Pencils					
4 Boxes		Staples - SF-1					
						TOTAL	

DELIVER TO: Mary Smith   BLDG. 1   FLOOR 2   REQUISITIONED BY: Mary Smith   DATE 8-1-66

RECEIVED BY: DATE   APPROVED BY: John Jones   DATE 8-1-66

EXHIBIT 2

the approval of the requisition. Very often a department head will pre-sign blank requisitions and allow departmental requisitioners complete freedom as to item and quantity requested. The overall control factor is the departmental budget; and as long as total charges to the department are lower than the budget, little or no supervision is attempted.

The completed original requisition is forwarded to the stores department. Usually this is accomplished through an in-plant mail system or by personal visits by the requisitioner to the store itself. Most companies recognize the value of time and are hesitant to allow workers to requisition material personally. One company estimates that a worker who earns $3 per hour must produce salable product worth ten times his hourly rate in order to generate a profitable return to the company. In this instance, the value of a requisitioner becomes $30 per hour or $.50 per minute. It is therefore extremely important to keep employees at maximum output at all times.

Upon receipt of the materials requisition, the stores personnel fill and ship the order to the requisitioning department. In all probability this is accomplished within a 24-hour cycle. Obviously, materials can be obtained almost immediately if required; but, in general, the store operates on a "delivery tomorrow" basis. Once the goods are transferred from stores inventory to the using area, proper notation of this fact is recorded on an inventory control card; and, as previously indicated, the accounting department then charges the requisitioner (or job) and credits the store inventory.

This buying and selling procedure continues until a reorder point is reached, and then the justification for stock replenishment is noted on a traveling requisition. Primarily, this form is used to eliminate the need to make out a purchase order request form to order repetitive materials. The most important features of the traveling requisition are the historical record of available sources of supply, the price paid, and the standard reorder quantity. A review of the traveling requisition from the standpoint of competitive vendor price levels indicates that price differentials from competitive suppliers will vary less than 5 percent. Another fundamental conclusion established by an objective analysis of the traditional procurement method, therefore, is: *the competitive nature of low-value repetitive materials restricts potential price savings to less than 5 percent between reliable vendors with equal-quality materials or services.*

Very often, traveling requisitions are maintained for materials even though the items are not repetitive enough to be physically stocked in a storeroom. A detailed analysis will indicate that approximately 50 percent of the plant needs are usually acquired direct from an outside vendor. As previously indicated, this is primarily the result of space and monetary limitations imposed on the store's facility. Therefore, we have another conclusion: *the availability of repetitive-use materials from a company-controlled inventory is approximately 50 percent of the total plant requirement.*

The request to purchase materials from an outside vendor is generated either by a direct purchase request form or by a traveling requisition for replenishment of store materials. An important principle is that *a need must exist and be properly authorized before purchasing can issue a commitment to buy.*

The distinction between buying and purchasing is clearly evident in terms of function and responsibility. Unfortunately, the majority of purchasing departments operate primarily as buying offices. The normal procedure followed by the purchasing department, once it has received authorization to buy, is first to find out what vendor (or vendors) sell the material requested. Most companies adhere to a policy of maintaining multiple sources of supply and refrain from specification by brand wherever possible. The most frequent explanation for multiple-source buying is that it creates lower prices and more dependable availability of plant needs.

An objective analysis of this policy has established a very startling finding: *the number of competitors within a given market area decreases as the value of the material to the productive capacity of the company increases.* While this principle may cause some concern with regard to protecting the plant needs, the question as to the overall importance of the need must be answered first.

Consider the need for stationery versus the need for a replacement part for productive machinery. There is no question as to the relative importance of these items; yet there are always many vendors of stationery supplies but usually only a few or even only one source of supply for the replacement part. Consider also the relative importance of utility services. Without electric power or natural gas, a company would have to curtail operations resulting in substantial losses; still companies seldom attempt to establish an alternate source of supply. One survey indicates that one national corporation recognized and issued orders to over 50 vendors for stationery supplies, but their production effort was standardized on one type of machinery.

In addition to determining what vendor can supply the materials required, purchasing is responsible for negotiating the actual price to be paid. This responsibility is very often a direct result of a control device established by the accounting department. The policy statement may require that all purchase orders issued by the company include a firm price commitment. This is designed to prevent a vendor from charging more than a fair price, and to eliminate the possibility of errors in invoicing.

This policy has created the "request for quotation" form used by many companies. Admittedly, on high-volume repeat items the policy is very loosely enforced, and most of the time the last price indicated on the traveling requisition is used for the purchase order price. In the event of a discrepancy between the purchase order price and the invoice price, the purchasing department is the determining factor inasmuch as price is its responsibility. Very often all incoming invoices are processed through the purchasing department prior to going to accounting in order to eliminate the possibility of price discrepancy between the purchase order and invoice. This practice greatly reduces the control factor usually associated with a system of departmental checks and balances.

The purchasing department determines which vendor will be given the order. One of the ways most frequently used is to base the decision on the lowest price. The buyer of repetitive materials seldom considers the comparative value of the vendors involved. Another method used very frequently by buyers is the "sequence selection" technique. This involves placing the order with the vendor on a turn basis—that is, Supplier A received the last order and therefore it is Supplier B's turn. This can only be used where the price differentials and vendor service are competitive.

Of course, other determining factors play an important role in vendor selection. They include financial responsibility, trade relations, personal relations, and engineering service supplied by vendors; however, these become less important when buying low-value materials.

Once the vendor has been selected, the next step in the reorder cycle is to issue the purchase order document. This is a multipart form designed to implement the overall acquisition of materials (and services). The majority of purchase orders consist of seven or more pages in various colors which designate the departmental flow of the forms. (See the flow chart in Exhibit 1.)

Invariably the original of the order is forwarded to the vendor. (A second copy may be included for a vendor acknowledgment copy which will be returned to the buyer by the vendor along with the expected date of shipment. This also serves to notify the buyer that the order has been received and accepted by the vendor.) Some companies are currently using the original order form as the acknowledgment copy by including a perforated section on the bottom of the document. This section can be easily torn off and returned to the buyer with the necessary information, and thereby one copy of the order set is eliminated.

Two copies (2 and 3) are usually forwarded to the proper receiving department to be used as checks against incoming shipments and to provide information as to who will ultimately receive the materials.

Another copy (4) is very often sent to the accounting department to keep it informed of the dollar commitment and also to provide it with pre-price information.

Two copies (5 and 6) are retained by purchasing as open order copies to be used for expediting late shipments and for back orders when they occur.

The most important information on a purchase order is the purchase order number. This number is the basic control mechanism used throughout the procurement cycle. The vendor is instructed to use the purchase order number for all references to the order, and very often files are kept on a numerical as well as an alphabetical basis.

The importance of a buyer's signature is greatly diminished when one surveys the number of confirming orders issued by the average company. In these instances, the materials are very often received in the plant before the confirming order is issued.

After the supplier has been notified of the order, either by receipt of the purchase order or by telephone, he proceeds to function as a point of supply. Without going into a great deal of detail concerning a vendor's activity, it is sufficient to note that he must perform in a manner which will generate a profit for his services. This includes stocking materials, maintaining adequate inventory records to prevent out-of-stock conditions, replenishing stock, shipping materials, and accounting for sales to customers.

The order is shipped by the supplier to the customer's receiving area along with corresponding shipping papers designed to provide proof that the customer has received the order as indicated. The purchase order number is the control factor and appears on the shipping papers and packages alike.

The receiving clerk verifies the count and condition of the materials in the shipment and signs the shipping papers accompanying the order as well as one copy of the open purchase order (Copy 3). This copy, along with a copy of the shipping paper is forwarded to accounting so that it will then have justification to pay the invoice when it is received from the vendor. Copy 2 of the open order is also signed by the receiving clerk and returned to the purchasing department in order to close its files on the transaction.

A signed copy of the shipping paper is returned to the vendor. This permits him to issue an invoice on a completed shipment. Very often the invoice is sent to the purchasing department for a preliminary check of terms and conditions in order to eliminate errors before it is turned over to the accounting department for payment.

Accounting is responsible for checking the mathematical extensions of the invoice and the price structure with the initial purchase order and then issues a check closing the entire transaction.

ANALYZING THE TRUE COST OF THE STANDARD METHOD

Much lip service is given by professional purchasing agents to EOQ and the "buy for value" concepts; however, in practice the vast majority of buyers consider price as the prime factor, and the total amount bought is based on an annual requirement. This is, as we have already pointed out, caused by the fact that national brand materials are recognized as competitive in performance as well as price and they hold their value well.

What have been overlooked in this approach to procurement are the excessive administration costs. The purchasing department may save a few dollars by taking advantage of a quantity discount price but give little or no consideration to the added cost of storing the materials. "That is somebody else's problem," is the usual response.

In order to establish the total *real* cost of procurement, an exhaustive study must be made of the entire procurement cycle. This is sometimes not practical and is of little value when it can be established that general and administrative burden costs exceed 200 percent in many major corporations.

Rather than attempt an exhaustive study, we can make a simple evaluation of a stores area. The basic information related to cost should include the following:

1. Number of items physically stocked.
2. Number of items in stores record control.
3. Inventory value.
4. Average value per item.
5. Frequency of turnover by item—by total value.
6. Percent out of stock.
7. Number of items obsolescent.
8. Value of obsolescence.
9. Inventory shrink.
10. Capital investment.
11. Insurance and taxes.
12. Number of employees.
13. Salaries of employees.

An example of a store area where one such cost study was made is shown in the photograph in Exhibit 3. This picture represents a stationery storeroom designed to provide availability of repetitive office supplies to a general administrative work area. This photograph is probably quite indicative of similar stores areas in most major companies.

Within this storeroom, 300 individual kinds of stationery supplies were stocked. There were many basic items such as pencils, file folders, paper clips, and envelopes. Each of these basic items has several variations, which inflates the total number of items stocked. For example, the users of pencils are not content with plain lead pencils; they also require red, green, blue, and so forth. In addition, they are not satisfied with one degree of hardness; they must have soft, medium, and hard pencils. Similar instances were found in file folders (left-hand and right-hand);

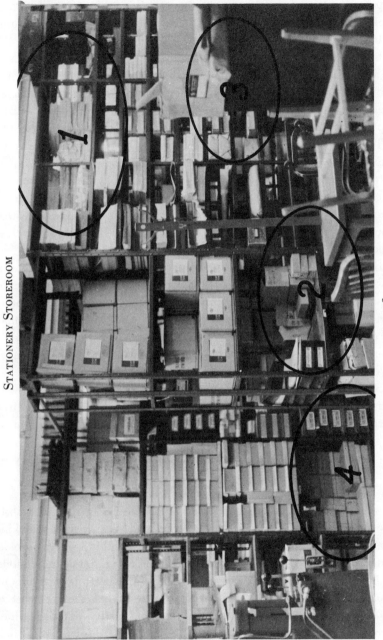

STATIONERY STOREROOM

EXHIBIT 3

paper clips (small and large); typewriter ribbons for every brand of typewriter; and so on and so on. The inventory analysis shown in Exhibit 4 gives an idea of the variety of items stocked.

In addition to the 300 items stocked, there were store record cards on an additional 200 items, many of which were bought frequently but not stocked because of their high value or low turnover. These included capitalized items such as typewriters or calculators which are seldom kept as store items but very often are included on the store record file.

The value of the inventory represented by this photograph was approximately $3,000, or an average of $10 per item. In reality, many items had an individual item value in pennies, but the total quantity stocked increased the value to a significant dollar amount. Ball-point pens had a value of only $.10 each but were stocked in dozen quantities. They were purchased, however, in multiples of one each and priced according to quantity bought.

By looking at the reorder history indicated on the stock record cards, it was evident that many items had a rapid turnover rate—for example, paper clips were purchased four and five times a year. On the other hand, many items were bought only once a year, and some less than once a year. It was also discovered that the lower-value item turned over more frequently than high-value materials. In total, the entire inventory turned over approximately two times in a year.

Stock-outs were virtually nonexistent in this particular storeroom. This is a tribute to the individual responsible for inventory control. Several other factors helped keep the stock-out problem to a minimum:

1. Availability of materials from local vendors.
2. Experienced suppliers who accurately anticipated company requirements.
3. High minimum reorder points.

At first glance, there seemed to be no problem with regard to obsolescence. This is because a person can't see obsolescence by just looking at a lot of items on a shelf. The photograph in Exhibit 3 shows obsolete materials, but one must know what to look for. Some simple indications, such as dust and discoloration are usually apparent; however, good housekeeping may hide them. In order to establish the real cost of obsolescence, an item-by-item review must be made. Materials which turn over less than one time per year are probably obsolete unless they

INVENTORY ANALYSIS

List of Supplies in Office Services Stockroom as of 3/27/61

Stock No.	Description	Usage for 1960	Inventory on Hand
0-500	Ball-point pens, assorted colors	12 gross	477
0-501	Dictaphone memo belts	2,000	2,100
0-503	Esterbrook dipless pen points #2556	0	33
0-505	Blank inserts—Globe Wernicke #AT144	12 pkgs.	5 envelopes
0-506	Esterbrook dipless penholder with pen points #2668	0	11
			20
0-507	Acopress binders 8½ × 11 red pressboard	300	125
0-508	Blaisdell Marxal leads #2073 black	0	48 boxes
0-509	Monroe adding machine ribbons, red & black	0	29
0-510	Star type cleaner #1226	24	23
0-511	Dictaphone pads #B545A	0	72
0-512	Multigraph pencils #40-2538	144	140
0-514	Pocket envelopes, 9½ × 11¾—Nibsob flat	1,000	355
0-517	Pads, yellow #7438 8½ × 13¼ legal-ruled	48	36
0-523	Burroughs adding machine ribbons, red & black	24	11
0-526	Copyflex paper developer #146P	48	0
0-527	Dictaphone pads #B63	72	72
0-528	Folders, full-cut manila, single top 11 Pt. 150 lb. stock #3043	10,000	0
0-529	Ribbons, IBM Executive P.S.M. new Model ⅝16 × 4 OD P-34 medium cutters—replacement for the	360	0
	Boston K5 pencil sharpeners	9	32
	Comptograph ribbon #44, red & black		14

EXHIBIT 4

can be classed as repair parts and are vital to production. Examples of obsolescence are indicated by the circled numbers in the photograph.

The area designated No. 1 represents $75 worth of reproduction paper. During the past year, the equipment for copy work was changed, and this paper was no longer needed. No notification was made to the storeroom prior to this change, and no attempt was made to work off the inventory. The original supplier of this material was not interested in accepting a return for credit because it had exceeded its shelf life and was then worthless. In addition, the vendor was most unhappy over the fact that a competitive material was being used rather than the product he had to offer and as a result considered this a lost account.

Area No. 2 represents the supply of pen points, which seemed endless at the current low rate of withdrawal. Although there were only three boxes involved, they did represent some dollar value. In addition to the pen points, there were two boxes of ink wells and one box of "executive type" penholders designed to hold the pen points.

Area No. 3 indicates a small storage cabinet which held bottles of blue ink which were obsolete because blue ink did not register on the copy paper when put through the old duplicating equipment. A study indicated that black ink would take an image; so the switch from blue ink to black ink was recommended. Again, no attempt was made to phase out the blue ink or sell it back, and consequently a quantity of unused blue ink was the result. Not shown is a cabinet full of black ink which had also become obsolete because the company had converted entirely to the use of ball-point pens. In addition, the new copy equipment can duplicate every color of ink.

Area No. 4 shows the location of imprinted envelopes which were no longer used as a result of a change in the corporate name. The corporate image warranted that the new name be used, and it would not have been proper to cross out the old name and type in the new identity. Here, also, it was almost impossible to sell the existing supply.

In total, the obsolescence represented in this one room exceeded $300, or 10 percent of the value of the inventory stocked. This is the basis for another principle often overlooked by management: *obsolescence is a significant factor when related to the materials which contribute to its existence.*

Usually obsolescence is related to an overall value such as total corporate net worth or total procurement dollars and, as such, is a rather small percentage. But what about the amount of obsolescence generated by commodities of major value? Should obsolescence, for instance, be charged against electric power or other utilities associated with the plant operations? These are major factors in figuring dollar expenditure, but it is virtually impossible to create obsolescence in this area. It is possible to waste electricity by not turning off the switch or to generate more steam than can be consumed; but this is waste, not obsolescence. Obsolescence is generated primarily in the MRO categories and, as such, they represent a much higher factor than has been previously acknowledged.

Inventory shrinkage is another very difficult area to determine. It is a polite term for theft. To say it does not exist is to refuse to face facts. The study of this stockroom did permit some indication of the extent of this problem. From an accounting standpoint, inventory shrinkage does not exist. There will always be a materials requisition or a store issue slip to justify the current value of the inventory compared to a previous level, but an analysis of the individual transactions may prove very interesting. Try to explain why there is a sudden upsurge in the usage of pencils, pads, rulers, and erasers during the last few weeks of August and the first few weeks of September. Every year prior to Christmas there is a heavy run on cellophane tape, but why is this so when papers are normally held together by paper clips or staples and not by tape? How much does this cost a company? This survey indicated a conservative $300, or 10 percent of the value.

Money tied up in inventory is not available for investment in a profit-generating area. Regardless of whether accounting refers to the materials stored as inventory or expense, the fact remains that the dollars involved cannot be used for any other purpose until the materials involved are consumed. How much is money worth to a corporation? A 5 percent return on investment is considered conservative and will serve as a reasonable value of the cost of inventory. This means that the inventory of office supplies represented in this case cost at least 5 percent of the total investment of $3,000—or $150.

Insurance and taxes can also be significant, but for the purpose of this discussion we will assign no value at all to the cost of inventory. Suffice to say that it does exist and should normally be considered.

In this particular storeroom, only one employee was involved on a full-time basis. The need for a store operator was created by the fact that there were a large number of transactions on a day-by-day basis. Someone had to be responsible for maintaining a proper assortment of items in the necessary quantity to prevent out-of-stock conditions and provide service to the users. The value of the materials stored in this room had little or no influence on how many people were required. The determining factor was the number of items and the number of transactions. The salary expense charged to this area was $4,500 annually. This included the fringe benefits usually associated with expense.

Admittedly, the salary paid this employee indicates a marginal responsibility and may be a contributory factor in the creation of obsolescence and shrinkage costs. However, the total dollars involved in these expenses amount to only $600, and this amount added to income would hardly improve the caliber of the employee.

A recap of the expenses generated by this one inventory of stationery supplies amounted to a total cost of $5,250:

Obsolescence	$ 300
Inventory shrink	300
Capital investment	150
Salary for one employee	4,500
	$5,250

When this expense is compared to the inventory turnover of approximately two times per year, the cost ratio generated is a staggering 87.5 percent.

Further analysis of this particular stationery storeroom showed that the requisitioner considered delivery within a 24-hour period excellent service. A delay of several days was considered normal and was of little concern to the requisitioner involved.

In addition to the storeroom represented by the photograph in Exhibit 3, five other stationery storerooms existed in buildings throughout the local plant complex. Each store maintained essentially the same type of materials and represented corresponding expense factors. At this point the amount of money connected with stationery stores began to become significant in that a $25,000 expense was required to provide an on-the-premises accessibility of materials that are available locally.

There are many other costs which must also be considered, such as the cost of the buyer's time, the typist's, the accountant's, and so forth.

All of these costs are created in whole or part by the number of transactions generated by the "system." Most companies refer to these factors as "burden" or "general and administrative expense." And we must remember that the objective of Systems Contracts is to create a technique designed to facilitate procurement of repetitive-use materials at a minimum of administrative expense.

ANALYZING THE TIME FACTOR

Our analysis has shown that only about half of the time can the user expect to get his needs on a 24-hour basis. The other half of the time he must wait considerably longer for the goods to arrive. For example, in metropolitan areas such as Chicago or New York, it is considered fast service if an order is delivered within six days. In the areas more distant from supply points, the time required to receive an order in the plant may increase to two weeks or more.

This is not to say that the purchasing department is responsible for delays but only that it is a contributing factor. Most delays are caused by the "system." It usually requires one working day for a purchase requisition to arrive in a purchasing department. The in-plant mail system may be a prime cause for delay if mail is picked up and delivered only at specified times. Once the request is delivered to the purchasing department, another one and a half to two days may be required to select the vendor and type out and sign the purchase order. If the order is mailed promptly, another 12 to 18 hours may be required for delivery to the vendor. The vendor usually needs at least two days to process an order, and another day will be required for shipping and receiving. A review of the total time required is as follows:

Write request, get approval, and mail to purchasing	1 day
Select vendor; type and mail purchase order	2 days
Vendor fills order and prepares shipping papers	2 days
Shipping and receiving	1 day
Total	6 days

Therefore, we can state another conclusion: *normal delivery of material from outside vendors requires six days from date of request.*

As a result of the time lag affecting almost 50 percent of the materials required by the plant, individual users have created emergency-use stocks to offset the possibility of not having enough material to do their job effectively. These small inventories are usually not considered as such by the accounting department because they have been expensed to the using department. The fact remains that they are stocks of unused supplies, and these inventories in total can exceed the value of materials classed as physical inventory.

ANALYZING TOTAL INVENTORY

As indicated above, inventories exist over and above those under inventory control, as defined by accounting. Again, consider a simple item such as a pencil. The individual pencil user requires one pencil at a time to write with. In addition to the one-pencil "work in process," there is a small work-in-process inventory in the top drawer of the user's desk or perhaps in a small container on the top of the desk. This inventory averages 12 pencils because pencils normally come packaged 12 pencils to a box, and one box is a standard request quantity. When the user's inventory position reaches a reorder point, his secretary replenishes the desk inventory from a supply of pencils probably located in a two-door file cabinet someplace in the office itself. The total number of pencils stocked in the subinventory usually does not exceed four or five dozen pencils, which is a few weeks' supply for the office. The office substock inventory is replenished from a building crib which in turn draws supplies from the central stores facility.

The total inventory position of available materials can be summarized as follows:

Work-in-process inventory	X	number of people
Substocks	X	number of area
Crib stocks	X	number of cribs
Central stores	X	number of central stores

It is readily apparent after an evaluation of the total inventory position that there is a considerable amount of safety stock throughout the entire plant facility. These safety stocks exist on virtually all repetitive-use materials simply because of the user's fear of being caught short.

Of even more importance is the fact that these inventories exist on materials carried in central stores as well as those purchased direct from outside vendors. The possibility of controlling all levels of inventory is not practical; therefore, most companies allow them to exist. In general, these inventories are sufficient to enable the user to continue his normal operation from one day to several weeks without requiring additional supplies from outside sources. Another conclusion: *point-of-use inventory of repetitive materials is sufficient to maintain normal operations for at least 24 hours.*

RATING OVERALL EFFECTIVENESS OF THE
STANDARD PURCHASE ORDER SYSTEM

From the preceding analysis of the way most companies control their repetitive-order problem, we can generally conclude the following:

1. Eighty percent of all purchasing activity involves repetitive-use materials of nominal value.
2. Company storerooms concentrate on high-volume, low-value materials and supply about 50 percent of the plant requirement on a 24-hour basis.
3. Availability of other than stores materials requires six or more days from receipt of goods to point of need.
4. Inventories exist over and above those under inventory control.
5. The cost of such a system is a major contributor to burden expense.

CHAPTER II

Systems Contracts: A Better Way

The preceding analysis of the standard, purchase order procurement system indicates that while it is well defined and controlled, it is in general a costly and sometimes inefficient method. The following analysis of the Systems Contract will provide a basis of comparison between the Systems Contracts concept and other methods of procurement. A discussion of the specific ways and means of developing Systems Contracts will be treated in later chapters.

CHOOSING THE VENDOR

When the decision is made to select a vendor for a Systems Contract, the following conditions must be taken into consideration:
1. The agreement will be long lasting.
2. Service will be exacting.
3. Product acceptance will rest with the user.
4. Continuance will depend on compliance.

By utilizing a formal means of vendor selection, we can increase the chances of success in the long run many times over those situations where personal feelings and emotion are predominant. When quotations' based on Systems Contracts are used to determine the proper vendor, the purchasing man should be careful to weigh all of the facts at his disposal. Often the vendor with the lowest price cannot perform the services required. Although the differential between competing vendors will probably be less than 5 percent, the overall potential cost savings may be 25 to 50 percent.

Occasionally a vendor will offer a Systems Contract to a customer as a means of improving their working relationship. Under these circumstances the vendor should be given every opportunity to develop his idea without competition. Nothing is more frustrating for a salesman than to spend a considerable amount of time and energy selling a new idea only to have a buyer offer the idea to his competitors. This kind of conduct has caused much concern among ethical vendors; consequently, the flow of new ideas from them has largely disappeared.

One additional factor to be considered when selecting the proper vendor is choosing a supplier that specializes in the materials to be covered by the agreement. We should not ask a mill supply house to sell stationery supplies, for example. It is better to have agreements with several vendors and have them familiar with the specific products they represent. If a vendor is a large seller of a particular commodity, he is also a large buyer of these same items and, as such, will automatically be in a position to take advantage of quantity discounts where they apply —and these price advantages will be reflected in the price paid by the customer.

IDENTIFICATION OF MATERIALS TO BE COVERED

Once the vendor has been selected, a detailed analysis should be made of (1) the general categories of materials needed by the company, (2) the items within each category, and (3) the varieties of each item to be covered by the agreement. This sounds like a formidable task at first, but most companies already have a great deal of information available. A vendor can be of tremendous assistance in this task and should have free access to such records as store cards, traveling requisitions, and closed purchase orders.

Store record cards should indicate those items which are considered critical by the plant as well as provide an accurate record of the rate of turnover. Very often instances will be found where the turnover rate indicates that the item is no longer essential and is, in fact, obsolete. One may also find that the store record cards are virtually useless because of poor administration of the file system.

Traveling requisitions are maintained on items of repetitive use regardless of their status as store items. The frequency of reorder may be significant and should be included in a catalog listing of the commodities to be covered under the Systems Contract.

A wealth of information concerning past activity is available to the vendor in closed purchase orders. Many times a vendor is totally unaware of items being bought from competitive sources. In addition, he may not have a true picture of total usage because he has participated in only the business which he was successful in winning from his competitors.

Some purchasing people feel that it is somewhat unethical to provide any kind of competitive information; however, since these records represent closed business, this should not prevent a vendor being given access to the file. It is very important that all the guesswork be removed wherever possible so that the vendor can develop a successful program based on all the facts.

Very often the supplier who is awarded a Systems Contract is the one with whom the bulk of past purchases was made. He will in all probability have a very accurate idea about plant needs because of this experience.

STANDARDIZATION REQUIRED

Once all the potential items for a Systems Contract have been identified, the next step is to determine brand acceptance. The buyer must be made aware of the fact that the only merchandise he will receive under a Systems Contract will be from those brands available from the vendor concerned. This actually forces a company to undertake a standardization program, which is very often long overdue anyway, especially in such simple categories of materials as stationery. From experience, I find that most users accept the fact that nationally branded materials are competitive. For example, there are three major brands of light bulbs. Each brand fits all standard sockets and fixtures; all have substantially the same life expectancy; and prices are virtually the same. Thus it is questionable whether brand preference should be a significant factor in this area. Moreover, by using this approach on similar materials, a company can make major strides toward standardization. Of course, certain materials must be considered by brands, especially where replacement parts are concerned. The problem of brand selection and standardization is simple to overcome where past association with the vendor has already accomplished acceptability of materials.

CATALOG OF MATERIALS

This is one of the most important phases of the entire Systems Contract concept. Once the categories and individual items have been determined and agreed upon as acceptable by all concerned, they are ready to be listed. The catalog is based on the "blanket order" technique of buying in that all of the items covered are identified. Because of the large number of items listed, it is far simpler to use a book type of catalog rather than a series of purchase orders. The catalog can be indexed and coded in such a manner as to allow someone to locate easily any item listed. Usually the drawing up of the catalog is the vendor's responsibility, but many companies cooperate with the vendor in the total cost of this phase. A sample catalog page will be found in Exhibit 5.

The first column indicates the catalog number assigned to each specific item. The number is assigned in numerical sequence and corresponds to the alphabetical and size listing of the item. Catalog numbers are sometimes assigned in such a manner as to allow additions to be made to the catalog without disturbing the existing sequence; for example, 5, 6, 7—10—15, 16, and so on.

The degree of sophistication of the catalog number should depend on the vendor. It is the vendor's responsibility to assign the catalog number and not the customer's. The customer may have established item numbers which the vendor can use, but most store numbers are not acceptable in a direct conversion because they have lost their original sequence. If the vendor has the responsibility to assign catalog numbers, he can also use these identification numbers for other customers. In

MATERIALS CATALOG PAGE

Catalog No.	Unit Packaging	Item	Size	Order Unit	Unit Price
		CARDS, INDEX (Cont'd)			
		ALSO AVAILABLE IN COLORS BOTH PLAIN AND RULED. COLORS ARE: BLUE, BUFF, CHERRY, GREEN, AND SALMON. TO ORDER USE AMERICAN BUSINESS GROUP REQUISITION NO. 2.			
		CHALK			
80	144	White		1 Box	.52
81	144	Yellow		1 Box	1.27
		CHEESECLOTH			
82		Five Yards		1 Pkg.	.42
		CLIPS			
83	12	Clamps, Ideal #1, Large	2½"	1 Box	.17
84	50	" " #2, Medium	1½"	1 Box	.23
85	1,000	Clips, #1, standard Gem	1⅜"	1 Box	.48
86	12	" , Binder #12	¾" wide	1 Box	.48
87	12	" " #15	1¼" wide	1 Box	.70
88	12	" " #110	2" wide	1 Box	1.30
		CLIPBOARDS			
89		Letter size		1	.32
90		Legal size		1	.34
		CORD			
91		White, for tying	½ lb. ball	1	.42
92		Brown #36 for mailing	½ lb. ball	1	.34
		CORRECTION FLUID			
93		Hesco	2 oz.	1	.36

EXHIBIT 5

certain instances, the customer may wish to assign a specific block of numbers to a vendor to designate the basic categories—for instance, all fasteners might be assigned numbers between 10001 and 19999. The first two digits will then refer to the category, which in turn refers to the vendor.

We should be careful about getting too much sophistication in this area. The objective is to simply locate an item numerically and alphabetically in the quickest way possible.

A unit packaging column is sometimes included in the catalog and is very helpful in ordering. This information concerns exactly how the material is packaged: for example, a box of clips may consist of 1,000 or 12 depending on the size ordered. Sometimes the pack is one each because the items are sold in units of one. This is true of such materials as pipe valves and fittings. Usually the pack is the same as the manufacturer's standard pack.

The description column should be complete in every detail. It should identify the exact nature of the material in the same manner as used on a purchase order. Manufacturer's identification numbers should be included in the description. Very often the general category covered is used as a heading for the description: for example, "CLIPS—PAPER" would include "85—Clips #1 Standard Gem 1⅜" and "87—Clips Binder #12¾." The requisitioner using such a catalog will know exactly what size of paper clip is available. In addition, he will also know what brand will be supplied.

The order unit column almost always lists a minimum of one each of the pack. It represents the smallest quantity available to the customer. Occasionally an item is sold by weight but is ordered in feet or length. This is true with steel and can cause some confusion; however, if we keep the order unit, pack, and description simple, the order unit can easily be determined.

The price column represents the negotiated price at which the vendor agrees to sell the described item in the order unit quantity. A more comprehensive discussion of price negotiation will be found in a later chapter.

It is very easy to index the catalog once the categories have been established and the individual items listed. The categories should preferably be included in the catalog in an alphabetical sequence. Once the catalog has been alphabetized, the catalog numbers can be established in an alpha-numerical sequence. The index can then be arranged so that the reader can locate all his needs without any difficulty.

Besides conveying the advantage of making it easy to identify the actual items covered by the agreement, the catalog can be used to reduce the number of copies of the purchase order. In the standard purchasing method at least one copy of the open order is used by accounting for the purpose of establishing firm prices. If we supply a priced catalog to those responsible for pre-priced information, it is possible to eliminate their copy of the purchase order. In the event of price changes, new prices will be provided. Until such notification, the prices shown in the priced catalog are considered firm. Experience shows that price changes on contract materials can be limited to a quarterly basis. For those companies employing a standard cost accounting system, the prices established in the beginning of the year can be compared to the prices listed at the close of the year.

As a general rule, three or four priced catalogs are all that are required to service a Systems Contract. These will be assigned to (1) the vendor, (2) the purchasing department, (3) accounting, and (4) auditing.

Where the catalogs contain confidential information, additional control measures should be instituted. In general, the catalogs will only involve nonessential material sold at fair market prices. The number of priced catalogs distributed to the plant should be restricted to only those who have a need to know prices. If too many priced catalogs are distributed, the chance of overlooking one or more catalogs in the event of price changes is greatly increased and may cause confusion at a later date.

There should be catalogs for use at the point of requisition. These are virtually the same as the priced catalogs except that the price column has been deleted. The requisitioner seldom has a need to know exactly how much an item will cost; when a need does arise, he can secure this information from purchasing. Primarily, the requisitioner is interested in availability of materials. This is, perhaps, the outstanding feature of the catalog in that it identifies all the items available to him from a ready inventory. Without this, most requisitioners have no method of determining what materials are actually on the shelf in the storeroom. The requisitioner often gains this knowledge of availability only after months or years of requisitioning supplies. If an item is listed in the catalog, the requisitioner can be assured he will receive his materials within the time specified in the agreement.

REQUISITIONING THE MATERIAL

The requisitioning points are the people who will be directly responsible for initiating materials requisitions for supplies covered under the contract. They are the counterparts of those presently involved with writing requisitions under a standard purchase order system of procurement.

Each department is issued a catalog of the materials available to it under the Systems Contract. Occasionally it is not too costly to provide each requisitioner with a copy for his own use, but where several requisitioners work in close proximity to one another a single catalog is often sufficient.

It is suggested that the authorized requisitioners be identified as such and a listing be made available to the accounting department. It will be necessary to keep the list up to date because of employee turnover, and the listing should be used as a control measure. The responsibility of enforcement should rest with the company and not with the vendor. The main objective of Systems Contracts from the requisitioner's point of view is improved service. Occasionally, someone may order supplies without his name being listed on the approved list. If there is a bona fide need, it is better to take care of the situation first and check for authorization later. The real control over the requisitioner is found in the approval signature.

Under the standard purchase order system, all requisitions are approved by someone in authority before the materials can be ordered. This same concept holds true under a Systems Contract. The requisition must be approved by some individual in a responsible capacity. He should be known to both accounting and the vendor and should be checked for compliance. Of course, the amount of verification will depend largely on the value of the transaction and perhaps only a spot check is required. The fact remains, however, that the purchase authorization point (PAP) is responsible for authorizing the need and is a major control point.

One of the benefits of Systems Contracts is that the importance of the PAP has been brought back into proper focus. Too many department heads allow their people to order supplies with little or no restriction. Many times, blank requisitions are pre-signed so that the requisitioners can make withdrawals from storerooms without bothering the boss. This leads to the creation of private hoards of materials which are subject to future obsolescence. The PAP should personally approve every requisition after it is completed regardless of the type of purchasing system involved. The materials ordered should only be the amount needed to maintain work levels on a practical basis and nothing more. If the vendor guarantees delivery and consistently meets his obligation in a dependable manner, the requisitioner will have no reason to order more than his normal needs.

The tendency of most companies is to utilize the same form currently used for requisitioning stores materials. Generally, this form provides for all the basic information required to order materials under a Systems Contract. By using a form already familiar to the requisitioners, we can prevent many errors. If a new form is required, the format of an existing form should be used wherever possible.

The size of the requisition form itself will depend largely on the number of lines required for ordering material. The method of ordering is simplified to the extent that only one line will be required for cataloged items and consequently an $8\frac{1}{2}$ by $5\frac{1}{2}$ size is usually sufficient. This size provides space to order eight items, which is about double the average number of items ordered on a standard purchase order.

A one-page requisition form requiring carbons to create additional copies is sufficient. Four pages are usually required for a Systems Contract requisition form. This means an original and three copies. When designing a new requisition form, it is suggested that each of the four pages be in a different color. This will simplify the distribution of the finished requisition. New types of papers can be used to eliminate the need for carbon paper. The carbonless papers work exceptionally well for this type of form and provide a legible copy through all four pages. It should be stressed that the Systems Contract materials requisition is designed to be handwritten, thus eliminating the time lost in typing requisitions. Those who complain about the inability to read handwriting, especially their own, learn to print exceptionally well when their job depends on it. Actually, in the old system someone has had to read the handwriting in order to type out purchase orders.

An example of a materials requisition form used in conjunction with Systems Contracts is found in Exhibit 6. This form contains all the necessary basic information required:

1. *Corporate identification.* The vendor in all probability will extend the Systems Contract concept to other companies and may become confused as to the company originating a requisition. This is especially true where several companies dealing with the same vendor adopt the Systems Contracts, even to the standardization of requisition forms.

2. *Charge number.* This is the budget or expense responsibility to which the value of the requisition is to be charged by the accounting department. There are several categories of account numbers so that the material can be charged directly to the proper classification.

3. *Vendor identification.* This is just as necessary as corporate identification because there will in all probability be more than one vendor involved in the total system. The word "TO" provides the heading where the requisitioner will insert the name of the vendor of the materials he is ordering. A requisition will be restricted to include only those items available from a single vendor. If more than one vendor is involved, a separate requisition must be made out for each. Generally, a maintenance man is able to order the bulk of his needs from one maintenance catalog; an electrician should also be able to find the bulk of his needs in an electrical catalog; and so on.

4. *Quantity and order unit.* This information should conform to the specifications as indicated in the catalogs. The order quantity will be one unit or multiples thereof.

5. *Catalog number.* This is the number which has been assigned each item. Where more than one item is ordered on a requisition, it is suggested that they be ordered in numerical sequence so that all catalog reference can be done with a logical progression from low to high numbers.

MATERIALS REQUISITION IN SYSTEMS CONTRACTING

CARBORUNDUM
MATERIAL REQUISITION

REQUISITION NO. 492

TO: A B C Supply Co

CHARGE
ACCOUNT NO. 1234
DETAIL NO.
SHOP ORDER NO.
TO E. A. NO.

Quantity and Unit Ordered	Catalog or Material #	DESCRIPTION	Vendor or Inventory #	Quantity Issued	Std. Price Per Unit	Actual Price Per Unit	Extended Value
10	83	Clamps Lg		10		.17	1.70
4	85	Clips Gem		4		.48	1.96
						TOTAL	$3.66

DELIVER TO: Alice Smith

BLDG. 1 FLOOR 2

REQUISITIONED BY: Alice Smith DATE 9-1-66

RECEIVED BY: Ann Green DATE

APPROVED BY: Jane Jones DATE 9-1-66

EXHIBIT 6

6. *Description.* If we use the catalog number for item identification, the written description can be kept to a minimum. A brief description should be used in order to provide a crosscheck of the item ordered against the catalog number. Very often, errors have been found where one number was incorrectly copied from the catalog and did not correspond to the description of the material ordered in the description column. When this occurs, the requisitioner can be contacted by the vendor for clarification, thus preventing a delay in receipt of needed supplies.

7. *Vendor or inventory number.* Many manufacturers have established commodity numbers on the items they sell, and these numbers can also be included as another crosscheck of the actual item required.

8. *Quantity issued.* The vendor will use this as a check to insure that the quantity shipped is the quantity ordered.

9. *Price per unit.* This will be the price as shown in the priced catalog. There can be no deviation from this stated price, except in rare instances by mutual agreement between the company and the vendor. The price per unit should conform to the order unit as indicated in the first column.

10. *Extended value.* This represents the total cost of each line of billing. The price per unit is multiplied by the quantity issued to get the extended value.

11. *Total.* The total value of the entire requisition is found by adding each line of billing represented in the extended value column. The total value is the amount which will be charged to the charge number indicated on the requisition. This also means that the requisition should be restricted to those items charged to a single account number. Various accounting procedures can be developed which will allow the expense to be charged to several responsibilities, but this is more difficult to administer since the overall value of each requisition is usually too small to be of significant importance.

12. *Deliver to.* The order will probably be delivered to a receiving area, but very often the receiving clerk will require instructions as to in-plant destination. Occasionally, the materials requisi-

tioned can be delivered directly to a point of need by the vendor, thus again improving service. Where this is possible, the exact location, building, and floor should be so indicated.

13. *Requisitioned by and date.* The person responsible for determining the need for materials signs his name to the requisition. This signature should be known to the person responsible for approving the need for materials. Several attempts have been made to correlate the requisitioner with specific pre-identified charge numbers, but this has proved difficult to administer because of the many numbers involved. It is suggested that the date the requisition is issued be noted in order to provide a check on elapsed time between order and receipt of materials.

14. *Approved by and date.* This is the person responsible for authorization of the order or PAP. He should be a salaried employee in a supervisory capacity directly responsible for the requisitioner and the expenses charged against the department or job. Again, the date of approval will pinpoint any delays that may occur.

Perhaps too much emphasis is given to control of expense in view of the relative value of the dollars involved; however, most large corporations operate on a departmentalized or job-cost basis and therefore require this type of information. Other companies have very simple cost control methods and charge everything to a single expense number which is later allocated on a percentage basis to the various responsibilities. In either method, approval points should be established in order to prevent overordering on the part of the requisitioner and to serve as a control point.

One of the major factors in inflating the true cost of goods sold is the tendency of buyers to order and charge more material than is required for a job. Under the Systems Contract concept, this problem can be virtually eliminated.

15. *Received by and date.* The person responsible for verification of the receipt of materials should sign his name to the requisition when the materials are actually on the premises. He is assuring all concerned that the count is accurate and that the shipment arrived in usable condition. By noting the receiving

date, a continuing check will be available for an appraisal of
the entire procurement cycle.

As has already been indicated, the requisition is designed to be hand-written. Once the requisition has been completed and approved, the original and two copies are forwarded to the vendor whose name appears on the requisition. The fourth copy can be retained by the requisitioner as a copy of the transaction. Various methods are used to forward the set of requisitions to vendors.

1. Daily mailing is one method which can be used in most instances. The requisition is forwarded through the mail to the vendor and usually reaches him within 24 hours. Frequently, mail picked up by 5:00 P.M. is delivered before noon on the following day. Consideration as to "real need" is the determining factor in any method.

2. Vendor-driver pickup is a method involving the use of the vendor's truck driver as the means of communication between company and vendor. The requisitioner forwards the three-part order requisition to a central point, such as the receiving department. Each time the vendor makes a delivery, the driver picks up the new orders. This method can best be used where the driver is employed by the vendor and is familiar with the system. It is almost impossible to use this method with outside truckers.

THE VENDOR FILLS THE ORDER

As has already been indicated, the most important control feature of the purchase order system is the order number. Under a Systems Contract, the set of requisitions will be received by the vendor unnumbered. No number was mentioned in our discussion of the characteristics of the requisition form. It is suggested that when developing a requisition form for use with a Systems Contract we leave room for an order number but that the use of a pre-numbered form be rejected. The vendor has the responsibility of assigning an order number to each set of requisitions and assigns this number in numerical sequence as the orders are received. The order number is shown on all three pages of each set received.

Consider the difference between a customer-assigned purchase order number and a vendor-assigned Systems Contract requisition number. In reality, both documents are orders for materials. The purchase order number is a number which designates the transaction. For example, in Purchase Order 932170B, the six numbers indicate only that the form was in this sequence as it was numbered during the printing cycle. The letter "B" probably stands for a corporate division or a purchasing agent's initial. The entire number is nothing more than a reference point and statistically quite unimportant.

The requisition order number assigned by the vendor under the Systems Contract concept has exceptional statistical value and provides improved control of the transaction. Note the example shown in Exhibit 6. Here the requisition number is 492. This number, when assigned by the vendor, tells everyone associated with the program that this is the 492nd order received by the vendor from the customer this week, month, or year. By assigning the number in numerical sequence as received, the total number of transactions to date by vendor is indicated. In reality, both numbers (the purchase order and requisition order) perform the same function—that of providing a numerical reference point; however, the Systems Contract requisition number is statistically more valuable than the purchase order number.

Vendor identification can be accomplished by requesting that the vendor stamp his name on each page of the requisition. It can also be secured through the use of the requisition number. One method is to assign a block of numbers (1000-9999, say) to a specific vendor; another is to use a prefix number or letter such as 8-492, the prefix indicating the vendor's number. In any event it is a good practice to have the vendor's name appear on the requisition to eliminate any question concerning the point of supply.

Pricing the order is the vendor's responsibility and is based on the price information shown in the priced catalog. Since the requisitioner does not have a priced catalog, all requisitions will be forwarded to a vendor unpriced. The prices are indicated on the original and the second copy of the order. It is not necessary to price the third copy. Usually, the pricing of the requisition is done by the vendor when the third copy is being used as a warehouse copy by the vendor's stock clerk to pick the order physically from inventory.

When the third copy is returned to the vendor's office by the warehouse, the price clerk can extend the value of the items being shipped, basing this on the information shown in the quantity-issued column. The total price is the total value of the order and should include all taxes, freight, and so forth.

Each set of requisitions represents a separate order, and the materials involved should be packaged as such. This is done very simply by utilizing such packaging materials as paper bags, plastic sacks, twine, straps, and boxes. Very often the standard order quantity will be a boxed item which may be of sufficient strength for shipment as is.

The original of the requisition order is shipped with the material and serves as the packing list. The number-three copy is affixed to the outside of the package and serves as the shipping paper. No other documents are required for the individual orders. Where the goods are forwarded by an outside truck line, the vendor can pack the individual orders in a larger container and make out one set of shipping papers for the entire shipment. The second copy of the set of requisitions is retained by the vendor for his record of the transaction. This is a deviation from the purchase order system wherein the vendor usually receives and retains the original document. It is very important as an accounting-control measure to have the original requisition form returned to the customer. The information on the second copy is an exact duplicate of the original and provides the vendor with all the facts concerning the transaction.

The vendor is responsible for selecting the method of shipment, and in the majority of cases it is his own truck. Where an outside trucker is used by a vendor, it is important that the trucker be made aware of the necessity for dependable, on-time delivery. One of the basic factors when considering vendor selection is his method of shipment.

Establishing a specified delivery cycle is very important to the requisitioner because he must know when to expect his order to be delivered in order to provide the necessary lead time. Usually, most vendors operate a Systems Contract on a 24-hour cycle, which is about par for requisitioning from a company storeroom.

When establishing delivery cycles, we must consider the actual need rather than the personal desire to receive immediate attention. Proximity of the vendor must also be considered, but only in the light of actual need. A vendor 300 miles away might be just as acceptable as one three blocks away from the plant for nonessential supplies.

The important element in setting up the delivery cycle is dependability. The requisitioners will be dependent on the ability of the supplier to deliver on time; and by meeting this obligation, the supplier will gain the confidence of the requisitioners.

When we establish delivery times, the supplier's truck should be given priority over nonscheduled deliveries. The quickest way to ruin an otherwise dependable delivery cycle is to keep the contract truck driver waiting every time he makes a delivery to a plant.

One of the major benefits of the Systems Contract concept has been the elimination of excessive numbers of trucks from delivery areas. Prior to this, trucks representing all the vendors and many orders delivered a small quantity of merchandise at a time. Now one truck will deliver a sizable quantity of merchandise per shipment because of the concentration on one or a few vendors for the bulk of the plant needs.

One method of informing the requisitioners of the delivery schedule for a contract is to note the schedule in the front of the catalog. It might also be suggested that a notation be made concerning what time the truck leaves the supplier's warehouse so that by knowing the departure time a requisitioner can make an addition to an existing order. The entire order can then be delivered on a regular delivery cycle and the possibility of an emergency shipment eliminated.

RECEIVING THE ORDER

The receiving function, under a Systems Contract, retains the same responsibility as under the purchase order system. The receiving department is responsible for verification of receipt of usable material. Some may wonder if Systems Contracts places a heavier burden on the receiving function as a result of the shipment containing many individual orders. The answer is no because, regardless of how many orders are involved, receiving is responsible for all materials coming into the plant and must, therefore, verify the total number of items received. In addition, the receiving clerk probably does not know, and will not, under a Systems Contract, count every item of every order. Spot checking of the received order is the rule to be followed. Another time-saver for the receiving function is the fact that the shipment will consist of standard manufacturer's packs, and it is much quicker to count one box of ¼″ bolts than 144 separate ¼″ bolts. It is also possible to establish receiving authorities within the areas of ultimate use. This will further expedite the receipt of materials and help reduce the number of transactions in a central receiving department.

Upon receipt of the materials, the receiving clerk verifies the count and acceptability of the material and forwards the shipment, along with the third copy of the requisition, to the requisitioner. The original of the requisition will be signed by the receiving clerk and forwarded to the accounting department. The ultimate verification of the acceptability of the order rests with the originator of the requisition; and unless there is a rejection by him, the order is considered "accepted" as received.

If a shipment is rejected, the vendor should be contacted and a replacement made immediately. No paper need be involved if an exchange of material is possible. The total elapsed time for the entire order cycle under a Systems Contract is usually 24 hours or less. The only delay in the cycle is the communication of the order from the requisitioner to the vendor. When this is done overnight, the effect of this time lag is greatly diminished. Where the vendor is in close proximity to the customer and utilizes his own delivery truck, the entire cycle can be reduced to a matter of a few hours or even minutes. The emphasis must always be placed on the "real need" in order to prevent the possibility of placing undue hardship on the vendor to perform for the sake of performing.

The receiving clerk verifies receipt when he signs his name to the original of the requisition. This document is then forwarded to accounting. At this point the requisition becomes the invoice under a Systems Contract. The basic information necessary to charge the using department for the materials ordered is indicated on the original requisition. By using the original requisition as the invoice document, all possibility of duplicate payment is eliminated.

Accounting may check the unit price with the contract price found in the priced catalog. There should be no difference, but if there is, the catalog price is the only price paid. Responsibility for price changes rests with the purchasing department upon proper notification by the vendor. As with the receiving function, accounting should spot-check received requisitions on a statistical basis rather than a total audit. In many instances the dollar value per requisition will be too small to warrant an intensive check. The next step will be to prove extensions and totals in order to correct any mathematical errors. Again, experience has proved that the errors tend to wash out in the overall program. Accounting is also responsible for proper signatures and should spot-check requisitioner and approval signatures.

The accounting department charges the total value of the order to the proper account number as indicated on the requisition. All materials ordered under a Systems Contract are "expensed as received" rather than charged to an inventory for later disbursement to using departments.

PAYING THE INVOICE

Another feature of the Systems Contract, which simplifies the overall transaction, is the "total payment" method of vouchering. Each original requisition is an invoice; but rather than issue a check for each transaction, the original documents are held for a specified period of time and then one check is issued covering all of the completed transactions. There are two basic methods used:

1. *Tally sheet.* The vendor prepares a listing, called a tally sheet, based on the dollar value indicated by the second copies of the requisitions completed during the specified pay period. The total value for each requisition is listed according to the numerical sequence of the requisition number and a grand total for all of the transactions completed during the period is shown. A sample of a tally sheet is shown in Exhibit 7. The vendor's name should appear on the tally sheet to prevent confusion when two or more contracts are in force. The accounting department makes a tabulation of the corresponding original requisitions indicated by the order number on the tally sheet. There should be no difference between the vendor's tally and the company's tally, since one is merely a duplicate of the original and therefore one check can be issued for the total amount. Emphasis should again be placed on the fact that all prices indicated under a Systems Contract concept are negotiated "F.O.B. delivered net," which again simplifies the entire transaction.

2. *Direct payment.* In this method, the accounting department

PD-70 7/62

SHEET ___ OF ___   **TALLY SHEET**   VCHR. NO. _____

                                                                                    PAYEE NO. _____

TO: THE CARBORUNDUM COMPANY   TERMS _____

                                                                                    PRICE CHECKED _____

PERIOD ENDING _____   DATE _____   EXT'N. CHECKED _____

REQUISITION NUMBER	DOLLAR EXTENSION		REQUISITION NUMBER	DOLLAR EXTENSION		REQUISITION NUMBER	DOLLAR EXTENSION	
							TOTAL		

EXHIBIT 7

accumulates the verified received original requisitions and issues a check for the total value on a periodic basis to the vendor without waiting for a tally sheet. The stub of the check indicates by requisition number the requisitions included in the payment, and the vendor can check to total payment by tabulating the corresponding number-two copies. The full value of the numerical-sequence method of numbering requisitions can now be fully appreciated. In the event that a requisition is lost, either by the vendor or by the customer, it will be apparent when making the monthly or periodic tabulation. When this does occur, the other party can supply a photocopy of the missing requisition which will serve to substantiate the transaction.

A SUMMARY VIEW

An overall view of the Systems Contracts procedures is shown in the flow chart in Exhibit 8.

Before proceeding further with some of the more advanced techniques of Systems Contracts, a brief analysis of its basic concept in relation to its objectives is in order:

1. *Improved service to the plant.* Systems Contracts provides a means whereby the vast majority of repetitive-use materials can be delivered within a normal 24-hour work period. This means that upward of 80 percent of plant needs can be provided by vendors under Systems Contracts as compared with approximately 50 percent through a company-controlled inventory. This is a 60 percent improvement in service.

2. *Adequate control measures.* Systems Contracts provides necessary pre-priced information, charge numbers, approved signature, and receiving verification in the same manner as a purchase order system. Additional control measures are inherent in the program and will be discussed in a later chapter.

3. *Work simplification.* Eliminated or reduced are store record cards, traveling records, request for quotes, bids, purchase orders, expediting letters, acknowledgment copies, shipping papers, invoices, and other general correspondence closely

Flow Chart of Systems Contracting Procedures

User:

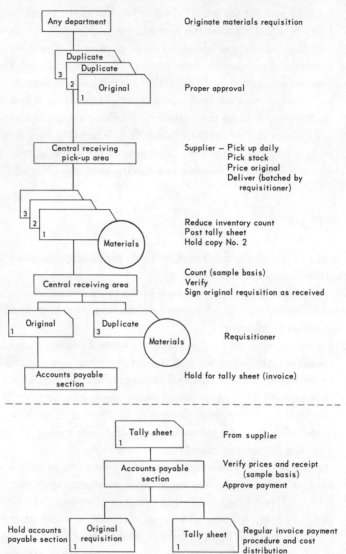

Any department — Originate materials requisition

Duplicate 3
Duplicate 2
Original 1 — Proper approval

Central receiving pick-up area — Supplier – Pick up daily
Pick stock
Price original
Deliver (batched by requisitioner)

3
2
1
Materials — Reduce inventory count
Post tally sheet
Hold copy No. 2

Central receiving area — Count (sample basis)
Verify
Sign original requisition as received

Original 1
Duplicate 3
Materials — Requisitioner

Accounts payable section — Hold for tally sheet (invoice)

Tally sheet 1 — From supplier

Accounts payable section — Verify prices and receipt (sample basis)
Approve payment

Hold accounts payable section
Original requisition 1
Tally sheet 1 — Regular invoice payment procedure and cost distribution

EXHIBIT 8

related to the procurement functions. In addition, sales calls by vendor representatives are greatly reduced, thus providing time for more important considerations to purchasing personnel.

4. *Reduction in administrative expenses.* Needless to say, many functions are by-passed under a Systems Contract. Without a storeroom, there is no need for a store clerk; without purchase orders, there is no need for a typist; and so on. To say that all of these functions can be eliminated is not practical, but the fact remains that the opportunity is there for a major reduction in personnel. Transactions create paper and paper creates people and people create expense which is reflected in reduced profit.

CHAPTER III

Special Situations

As we have already indicated, Systems Contracts can reduce costs when applied to known needs. However, the concept can be adapted to handle "unknown needs" as well.

The materials listed in the catalog represent those items stocked by the vendor for immediate delivery to the customer. They are the large-volume repetitive items and are easily identified in advance. We know from experience that many purchases involve items which may only be required once or twice a year or less. This is especially true with replacement parts or for job-shop operations. Since the use history is often inadequate, many items are not included in the catalog. If every possible need were to be included, the Systems Contract catalog would be too bulky and far too costly to produce and maintain. In addition, the cost of identifying every need would be prohibitive. By not including these materials in the catalog, yet allowing for their acquisition, the Systems Contract concept can cover approximately 90 percent of the total needs of the plant.

When the requisitioner has a need for an item or items not listed in the catalog, he should determine the general category of materials involved: cutting tools, plumbing supplies, electrical supplies, bearings, stationery supplies, and so on. By knowing the contract vendor who is responsible for the basic category, the requisitioner can assume that the supplier will be able to handle the noncataloged item as well.

Once the requisitioner has determined the probable source, the order for noncataloged material may be requisitioned in the same manner as cataloged items. The major difference will be in the identification of the material. Since no listing is made, there is obviously no catalog number to indicate exactly what material is required. Without a catalog listing, the description must be accurate in every detail to prevent error. It is suggested that noncataloged materials be ordered on a separate requisition; however, many companies do allow these items to be ordered along with cataloged materials. The determining factor will probably be the value of the material involved, order frequency, and the individual's responsibility. Approval and vendor notification are the same as for cataloged materials.

When noncataloged materials are ordered, the vendor must indicate this fact by adding the letters "NC" to the requisition order number. Thus requisition number 492 in Exhibit 6 will become 492 NC to indicate noncataloged materials are involved.

One of the problems facing the vendor in this situation is the ability to deliver the materials within the specified time period. It would be unfair to expect a vendor to provide the usual contract service on items of infrequent usage when he has not been alerted in advance to have the materials in stock. Chances are better than 50-50, however, that he will have the items in stock if the materials are of a standard nature because other customers serviced by the vendor may be large consumers of these items. When the vendor cannot supply within the normal contract cycle, the noncataloged materials must be differentiated from the cataloged materials and requisitioned on a separate order. This will prevent delay in shipping the standard items. When this is necessary, the vendor should contact the requisitioner and discuss the order with regard to actual need and availability, and a decision can then be made by the requisitioner as to whether the vendor can perform within an acceptable time period. One of the major topics to be discussed when negotiating a Systems Contract is the timing for delivery of noncataloged materials. Usually one to two weeks is considered adequate to acquire most standard materials from a manufacturer, but on nonstandard items, the lead time may run into several months. The requisitioners are notified of these lead times in advance and therefore should take them into consideration when planning their work.

As indicated above, when an item cannot be shipped and is included along with available materials on a requisition, the noncataloged material is red-lined from the original order. This requires that a new requisition be written to include the noncataloged material which will be shipped at a later date. The vendor should be provided blank requisition forms in order to allow him to re-write the order on the proper document. When a new order is written, the requisition number will become 492 NC-1. The numeral "1" indicates that the original requisition 492 NC authorized this transaction.

Prices for noncataloged materials are based on the vendor's standard selling price. Systems Contract vendors must be unquestionably ethical in their business conduct and as such should be treated fairly. What vendor having a Systems Contract worth many thousands of dollars would take a chance by charging an exorbitant price on a few transactions? Where the value of an individual item becomes significant, these items should be purchased through the normal purchasing channels and not included in a Systems Contract agreement. One way to police this activity is to establish a maximum dollar limit to the agreement.

The shipping and receiving functions are exactly the same as for cataloged materials, but the accounting function differs slightly. The control factor for accounting is the requisition number and the "NC" identification alerts the accounting department that the material cannot be verified in a pre-priced catalog. Usually the values are quite small, and a rule of thumb can be established where all items with an extended value of less than $10 will not need to be price-checked with the vendor. Where the extended value exceeds $10, the requisition is forwarded to purchasing for approval. The purchasing department in turn contacts the vendor and establishes the fairness of the price indicated on the requisition. The purchasing agent then signifies his acceptance of the price by initialing the requisition and forwarding the original back to the accounting department. From this point the transaction is completed as for cataloged materials.

Periodically, the purchasing department should review all of the "NC" transactions in order to determine if additions should be made to the catalog. When certain items begin to show frequent usage, the vendor should be alerted to put these in stock and thus provide better service. Most companies find that a quarterly review of requisitions and an annual updating of the catalog are adequate. Where a few items are involved, a letter of notification to all concerned is all that is required to update existing catalogs.

SPECIAL ORDERS

Special orders are the rush orders and emergency shipments which plague most companies. They require immediate attention on the part of all concerned because of the potential effect a shortage of material may have on production. Many purchasing departments spend the majority of their time expediting open orders in order to prevent late shipments. The fact that suppliers have not performed satisfactorily in the past is quite apparent from the size of the company storerooms. Under the Systems Contract concept the vendor must perform or lose the business. As soon as confidence in the supplier is gained by the requisitioner, the number of rush orders virtually disappear.

As for emergency situations in which no one can foretell when a certain material will be required, the Systems Contract concept provides a means for distinguishing between a "real emergency" and a "personal want." All too often, rush orders are merely a reflection of a requisitioner's lack of confidence in the supplier. The basic responsibility of the requisitioner and the approval point is to (1) determine the *real* need and (2) determine total need.

This means that the requisitioner must remain objective as to when he must have the material to do the job, and then he must also limit his order to only the quantity required. A requisitioner or a purchasing agent may inflate the size of an order when faced with an emergency as an additional hedge against future situations.

Where the vendor does perform according to the terms of the agreement, most emergency shipments have been caused by actual breakdowns which were totally unforeseen. When these do occur the Systems Contract concept provides a means whereby the plant can contact the vendor immediately on a direct basis for help.

The vendor must have all cataloged materials physically in stock. In addition, he must know how to replenish his inventory quickly in order to protect the customer against abnormal fluctuations. As the program progresses, more accurate forecasting of normal demands will be possible as a result of the close working relationship between the vendor and requisitioner.

In the event that an emergency does arise, the requisitioner is allowed to communicate an order direct to the vendor and specify "special handling." Several methods of communication are possible and include the telephone, TWX, and personal pickup.

The requisitioner may telephone direct to the vendor and indicate the quantity and description of the materials required. The control mechanism in this type of transaction is the charge number, and the vendor will request this information when he receives the call. In order to facilitate telephone orders, the customer should furnish blank requisition forms to the vendor. All the basic information pertaining to the requisition is available to the vendor under normal situations, and the only thing missing will be a bona fide requisitioner or approval signature.

TWX orders are handled in much the same way as telephone orders, except where there is a written, rather than a verbal, communication. The sender's copy may be retained by the requisitioner as future justification of the transaction.

Occasionally a requisitioner will send someone to pick up material from a vendor. When this is required, the set of requisitions should be made out in advance and left with the vendor. The vendor issues the material required immediately, and the person making the pickup signs the original requisition as the receiver. The vendor then mails the original requisition to the company accounting department as a completed transaction for payment in the normal manner. The third copy can be sent with the goods to the requisitioner.

Prior to placing the telephone call or sending a TWX, the requisitioner must decide the true nature of the emergency. Once it is determined that an emergency exists, the vendor should ship the needed material immediately regardless of costs. This means that various methods of transfer such as taxis, special trucks, and salesmen's cars can be employed as a means of delivery. The materials will probably be delivered directly to the point of need and may require some special handling as regards the receiving signature. This can very easily be secured by establishing receiving authorities in various areas.

As indicated above, an emergency order will undoubtedly involve increased costs to the vendor because of the very nature of the transaction. An emergency may occur after business hours and may require the vendor to work overtime. This eventuality (after-hours service) should be foreseen during the negotiation stage of the contract and special after-hours telephone numbers provided to the plant people involved. It is not reasonable to expect the vendor to absorb these excess charges as they would tend to reduce his margin of profit. The standard contract prices do not offer compensation for emergencies.

All emergency charges should be added to the extended total price shown on the requisition and be charged against the department responsible for the material. This provides a very effective method of limiting the number of emergency orders. Once the requisitioner is aware of the fact that he will have to pay for special service, he begins to think in terms of the next regular delivery, with the result that the emergency no longer exists.

We must always keep in mind that the materials covered by Systems Contracts are readily available from a supplier and, in addition, are probably maintained on the company premises in a substock or work-in-process inventory by more than one person. Second, the vendor's location is usually within reasonable distance of the plant, and he can deliver the goods in a matter of minutes when required to do so. Proximity is one of the deciding factors in vendor selection. It is difficult to justify the merit of maintaining company stores simply to protect against an emergency situation which can be handled just as quickly by an outside source of supply.

ADDITIONS TO ORDERS

Frequently, a requisitioner will discover a need for additional material after he has already forwarded a requisition to a vendor. When this occurs, the requisitioner may telephone the vendor and instruct the supplier to make an addition to the original order. The requisitioner should also add these items to the fourth copy of the transaction which he has retained for future reference. By permitting the requisitioner to contact the supplier immediately by telephone when the need arises, the end result will be that service to the plant is again improved.

Occasionally the add-on material may be a noncataloged item which is not immediately available from the supplier. If the material is to be delivered at a later date (and the requisitioner agrees to the delay), the vendor will make out a new requisition relating to all the basic information and assign a requisition number in numerical sequence as for normal transactions.

All shipping and accounting procedures are exactly the same as for normal transactions. Control of this type of activity is possible by noting how many additions are made during a pay period. When it appears that some individuals have a tendency to increase their basic order frequently, they should be required to justify their actions. Usually this is done by a department head. Any requisitioner who does not have a satisfactory explanation during such a review is subject to proper reprimand. In any event, the mere fact that the requisitioner is challenged has a marked effect on improving requisitioning habits.

PARTIAL SHIPMENTS

One of the greatest problems which face purchasing today is the staggering number of partial shipments. Systems Contracts can virtually eliminate the partial shipment problem because all orders are shipped complete and only immediate needs are required.

The major contributing factor to partial shipments is the unexpected order. Consider a supplier with 100 items on the shelf who receives an order for these same 100 items. It is possible for the supplier to fill the order, but not practical. He must consider his other customers who may have a requirement for some of this material before the stock can be replenished. The supplier cannot take a chance on being out of stock. He also knows that the customer does not need 100 items now but rather that this quantity is an EOQ which will last for a period of days, weeks, or months. By shipping part of the order now the supplier can satisfy the immediate needs of the customer and at the same time protect the potential needs of his other accounts. When the vendor's replenishment stock arrives, he can then ship the balance of the customer's original order. The customer tolerates this activity because he has become accustomed to it and because he is able to force the supplier to extend the price on the partial shipment to be based on the original quantity.

Suffice to say that the acceptance of a back order will mean creation of a considerable amount of additional paperwork. However, under a Systems Contract all orders are restricted to individual or departmental short-term needs. The possibility of creating an out-of-stock condition on this type of transaction at the supplier level is remote. Consider the same example of a supplier's stock of 100 items. A requisition is received for 10 items for immediate shipment. The remaining 90 in the supplier's inventory will be more than ample to satisfy the vendor's total customer needs.

The possibility is always present that a supplier may actually run short and not be in a position to fill a requisition in its entirety. When this occurs, the vendor has the responsibility to notify the originating requisitioner of the shortage so that the requisitioner is aware of the situation. If it went no further, this would represent an improvement over most existing methods of procurement because the user has been alerted to an existing problem within a few hours rather than days. He is now in a position to take immediate action to offset the potential delay.

An example of such a situation might be represented by a request for ten cataloged items. The vendor discovers that he only has five in stock and therefore telephones the requisitioner to apprise him of the situation. At this point, the requisitioner may determine that five will be sufficient. If this is the case, the vendor crosses off the figure 10 and inserts the figure 5 in the quantity-ordered column. The price extensions will be in accord with the quantity ordered because the extensions are based on the quantity-shipped column. The order is therefore shipped complete.

In the event that the requisitioner eventually requires the five units in addition to the five available for immediate shipment and is willing to wait, the vendor again crosses off the 10 and inserts 5 and ships this order as complete. The vendor then makes out a new set of requisitions containing all of the information shown on the original set. Where the vendor has access to copy equipment, he can make three machine copies of the original document, which can be used as reorder forms. The five items for future delivery to complete the original request are then shipped on these papers as soon as they are available. The control mechanism in this type of transaction is based on the requisition number. The vendor refers to the original set of requisitions and uses that number (say, 492) as the file reference. By adding a "1" the number for the reorder transaction will be 492-1. This indicates that order 492-1 is justified by order 492 and this is the first shipment of the back-ordered material. In the event that additional shipments are required, the numbers are again assigned in numerical sequence: 492-2, 492-3, and so on. This method gives purchasing and other interested parties a valuable tool for evaluating vendor performance. When requisition numbers change in this manner, a conference may be in order to check on the reasons why the vendor is not living up to the terms of the agreement.

The requisitioner should expect that his normal orders for cataloged materials will be filled without delay by the vendor. When the requisitioner indicates that he must have his materials immediately, the vendor must perform. These instances are quite rare, but they do occur and do require that the vendor use extraordinary means to satisfy the requisitioner. Some vendors buy the required materials from a competitive supply house. This may involve a change in brands, but in the event of an emergency the requisitioner will usually accept any brand that meets the basic specification. In this circumstance all increased costs such as air freight, special delivery charges, higher price, and so on are born by the vendor, and only the price shown in the catalog can be charged.

REJECTED MATERIAL

Occasionally, materials are delivered to the receiving department that are unusable because of breakage. The receiving clerk should contact the supplier by telephone and request an immediate replacement. The damaged materials can be exchanged for the acceptable materials, and the receiving documentation is then made as a normal transaction. Very often the original requisition is signed and forwarded to accounting before the materials are physically replaced.

Materials are sometimes rejected by the requisitioner for various reasons such as wrong material, not up to specification, change in plans.

When the requisitioner rejects the material, he contacts the supplier, who in turn replaces the rejected items with acceptable ones. Except in rare instances, no paperwork should become involved, and the original receiving report which was signed by the receiver continues to act as the invoice copy in accounting.

In the event that major dollar amounts are involved in a rejected order, the vendor may be reluctant to make an adjustment. When this occurs, purchasing should enter the picture and handle the situation in the same manner as a normal rejection. These instances are very rare but can and do happen.

CHAPTER IV

Benefits to All Concerned

The advantages of any new program must be evaluated in the light of the existing method. Based on the standard purchase order method, Systems Contracts provides many benefits through elimination, reduction, or improvement in the total plant operation. Perhaps the most difficult task is to assess the value of Systems Contracts in dollars and cents. Let us look first to the advantages it offers the buyer.

Paperwork. This is the area where reductions are most obvious because the original document (the materials requisition) is sufficient for the entire order cycle. The requisition is the order paper, the shipping paper, the receiving report, and the invoice. It eliminates the following:

1. Traveling requisitions.
2. Purchase order requests.
3. Vendor quotation requests.
4. Purchase orders.
5. Acknowledgments of purchase orders.
6. Expediting letters.
7. Receiving reports.
8. Individual vouchers.

Order error. Much of the problem surrounding the receipt of wrong material is the result of clerical error. The possibility of error is increased by the number of times an order is rewritten. The handwriting of one person may be difficult to read and a mistake in typing may occur. Unfortunately the mistake is often not discovered until several days have elapsed or until the time when the material arrives in the plant. Under the Systems Contract method, the error factor is virtually eliminated because the requisitioner and user deal directly with one another. In addition, the catalog number can be used to verify the description of the material ordered. In the event that the wrong material is received, the time elapsed is relatively short (usually 24 hours or less), and the vendor can be called upon to make an immediate adjustment.

Inventory. Systems Contracts will mean a twofold reduction in inventory: the number of items stocked will be reduced and the amount of dollars invested will be substantially less.

In general, inventory reductions in excess of 80 percent of the total number of items previously stocked are possible to attain. There is no need to maintain a company-controlled inventory of nonessential material that is merely a duplication of a vendor's warehouse. Once the program becomes operational, people gain confidence in the dependability of the supplier and a decided reduction in departmental substocks follows.

Coupled with the reduction in the number of items stored, there will be a reduction in capital investment. The percentage of saving here will probably be somewhat less than the percentage of item reduction because of the relative value of the material eliminated versus the material retained. Most of the physical reduction will involve low-value readily available MRO supplies. The material retained will consist of high-value replacement parts or items such as special cutting tools and jigs. The only practical way to determine the amount of dollars to be regained is to evaluate the existing facility. The money regained can be used by the company to invest in profit-generating areas.

Floor space. In many companies this is one of the most valuable aspects of the entire program. It is extremely worthwhile for a manufacturing operation to be able to regain 10,000 or more square feet of floor space. Prior to Systems Contracts, Carborundum had approximately 12,000 square feet of prime manufacturing floor space devoted to a central stockroom. This was an "expense" operation. Today this same area consists of production machinery and is now a "profit center."

Store records. Once the material has been physically removed from a store inventory, the corresponding store records can also be eliminated.

Many store facilities stock well over 20,000 individual items; by eliminating 80 percent of the inventory, it is possible to eliminate 16,000 records as well. In addition to the records, one should also consider the number of entries required to maintain an accurate chronicle of the transactions. One of the fallacies of record keeping is its actual value. For example, who cares exactly how many No. 2 black lead pencils were used last year? The records are maintained but seldom used. The real question is how many dollars were spent on stationery.

Obsolescence. By reducing the store inventory position to a minimum level, obsolescence will drop accordingly. Obsolescence is created by change, but very often changes would be delayed if the cost of change were properly evaluated. Admittedly, the vendor will have material which is subject to obsolescence; however, on standard materials he has the potential of selling them to other customers or of returning them to the manufacturer. In the event that the quantity of standard items stocked for the customer is unusually excessive, the vendor can and should expect protection from obsolescence. In addition, all nonstandard materials should be indemnified by the customer against loss to the vendor. If we identify excessive stocks and special items, these materials will be given proper attention when new techniques are considered. The cost of obsolescence will then become a known factor in determining the economics of a change.

Inventory shrink. Exactly how much can be saved in this area is unknown, but the mere fact that the materials are no longer available from a "company-owned store" will go a long way toward cutting this expense. Proper emphasis on the responsibility of supervision to substantiate as well as approve the requisitioner's needs is essential in controlling this problem, and the Systems Contract concept can do this very nicely.

Taxes and insurance. Depending on the area, the amount of money saved here can be significant. The reduction of physical inventory will obviously result in corresponding reductions in taxes and insurance.

Service. Above all, the improvement in delivery of materials to the plant is the most significant benefit of the Systems Contract concept. The ability of plant people to receive their needs on a dependable basis in a matter of hours means a more totally efficient production operation. The knowledge of what materials are available from a given source of supply is a valuable tool when planning work schedules. The availability of additional help in the form of value analysis studies from contracted vendors has also been of incalculable value in terms of man-hours saved.

Purchasing effort. Perhaps this is the one area of benefit least understood, especially by purchasing people. They see only the elimination of their empire as a result of the drastic cut in the number of purchase orders issued.

I believe the time is past when a purchasing agent can justify his value by the number of orders signed or the people he supervises. Today the purchasing department must become a profit center and divorce itself from routine paper handling and concentrate on cost reduction.

The elimination of the majority of purchase orders issued by the Systems Contract concept will mean "time" to the purchasing agent. He will be able to convert his time into more effective use. He will now be able to:

1. Plan and develop intensive value analysis programs.
2. Concentrate on major-dollar procurement.
3. Do a more effective job in expediting critical needs.
4. Analyze make or buy decisions.
5. Undertake the responsibility for all dollar commitments in areas such as advertising, capital expansion, and corporate acquisition.
6. Improve the value of reporting to management through use of more accurate knowledge of departmental expenses.

In short, the purchasing agent can become a manager in the true sense of the word rather than an overworked clerk.

Personnel. When considering the advantages of Systems Contracts, the potential savings related to personnel adjustment must be considered. Throughout this entire discussion, many areas for reduction in personnel are apparent. To not mention this as a potential cost reduction would be ridiculous. Quite frankly, the most significant financial benefit is often found in the reduction of the personnel. This does not mean that these reductions can be realized immediately upon signing the first contract, but they are possible after two or three are in force. This phase of the program may require several months or a year to accomplish, and it is quite possible that no one will be eliminated.

One should not become alarmed at the possibility of eliminating certain positions. In all probability, those areas most affected will be clerical positions such as typists, file clerks, inventory clerks, stock clerks, and price clerks. The people in these positions can be upgraded or retained during the period of implementing Systems Contracts—and without much difficulty. In addition, normal employee turnover will in all probability preclude any major personnel reductions. When someone leaves, his position can be consolidated with another, or a job may be abolished after a person retires.

Miscellaneous. Many additional benefits are also possible, such as reduction in the number of trucks making deliveries to the plant. The number of sales calls, not only on purchasing but also on various plant personnel, will be drastically cut. How important is a routine sales call? What benefit is there to the company? Time is our most valuable commodity; yet it is wasted when we permit routine sales calls which have nothing to offer other than a personal visit. By eliminating routine sales calls and channeling all plant contact through purchasing, the value of the sales presentation will greatly improve, and more time will be saved in the prime production areas. When a salesman does present something of value, more time can be devoted by all concerned for a proper evaluation.

Benefits to the vendor. In order for any program to be successful, it must be acceptable to all concerned. Systems Contracts provides many benefits to the vendor and helps reduce his costs and improve his return on investment.

As indicated above, the salesman's effort will become more productive because routine calls will not be required. Of more importance will be the fact that the salesman can devote the majority of his time to new materials or items not covered by the contract. These materials will usually consist of high-value items which return a significant dollar profit. In some situations, the person who services the contract is different from the one who calls on the purchasing department. This will allow the vendor to make a distinction between a high-cost sales effort and a relatively low-cost service man.

If the vendor performs in a satisfactory manner, there is no reason why he should ever lose a contract. Over the course of several months or years, a strong working relationship will develop between the vendor and the customer which will put the vendor on a first-call basis for all expansions and improvements involving his product lines. He may even be given the opportunity to expand into new product categories which in turn will increase his sales volume.

The sale is confirmed for as long as the vendor-customer agreement remains in effect. Needless to say, the vendor cannot take a complacent attitude toward a contracted customer because his competitors will not let him. His sales effort can be changed from one of routine solicitation to one of productive service. It is a well-known fact that the majority of a salesman's time is spent "behind the wheel" or "waiting to see." Under the Systems Contract, the salesman will visit directly with the users and discuss their mutual needs. Little or no time is lost, and the dollar return is many times greater.

Most vendor inventories are based on anticipation of future sales with customers. Very often the inventory levels are little better than good guesswork. The vendor's profit is generated as a result of inventory investment turnover. The advance product knowledge available to a vendor during the planning stages of a Systems Contract is extremely valuable to a vendor and will help him do a better job of inventory management. During the course of the contract the vendor can make necessary adjustments in his inventory based on updated information concerning trends and usage patterns which will be discussed with him.

Some vendors have expressed a fear that their dollar investment in inventory will have to be increased substantially as a result of a Systems Contract. This may be true; however, since the investment is the basis of earnings, it is to his advantage. By comparing inventory dollar investment as a percentage of sales, the percentage will in all probability be lower because of the increased turnover and better control of those items kept in stock.

The receipt of orders from the customer will fall into a routine pattern which will mean a saving in clerical time. The time-consuming effort required to price every line item will be simplified through the use of the pre-priced catalog. The need to make out shipping papers and the reference to purchase order numbers are eliminated. Packaging becomes a very simple process utilizing such things as paper bags, plastic sacks, wire tags, small corrugated cartons, and standard manufacturers' containers.

The contract vendor will recognize an increase in the total dollar value of each shipment. Instead of making a delivery of one or two cartons, he will probably deliver a sizable quantity of merchandise because he is now a preferred source of supply. Where special deliveries at the request of the company are required, he will be paid for any increased expense rather than giving it away to "hold on to a customer."

A simple monthly or periodic tally is all that is required. This can be furnished by either the customer or the vendor, and a simple tab run will justify the totals. All prices are quoted F.O.B. net delivered to the customer's plant, thus eliminating a great deal of mathematical confusion.

Having established that there are mutual benefits to be gained in Systems Contracts, we can move on to the next step of actually writing a Systems Contract.

CHAPTER V

Writing a Systems Contract

The basic ingredient in developing any successful program is the backing of decision-making management. Without this, it is virtually impossible to overcome the resistance to change inherent in every major company. The changes brought about by the Systems Contract concept are definitely in the corporate interest, but many little empires are likely to be in jeopardy. Some jobs are going to be eliminated or reoriented in such a manner as to affect the individual, and this almost always results in a negative attitude. In some instances even people not directly affected by the program attempt to prevent adoption because they fear that their department might be next. Therefore, top management must impose its authority. Then the objectives must be clearly defined, and major emphasis must be given to the communication of these objectives to all concerned.

Where the corporate policy is too vague or does not allow for adoption of the Systems Contract concept, it will have to be revised accordingly. A simple statement of fact is usually sufficient, accompanied by a flow chart outlining the basic procedure. Where a more detailed policy is required, the order procedure, requisition form, tally sheet, and so forth can be included.

Once the decision has been made to adopt the Systems Contract concept, even on a test basis, proper responsibility for installing the program must be assigned. This can be done in several ways, but the more successful programs have been developed by the purchasing department. Since the concept is fundamentally a method of procurement, this is the logical group. Occasionally management is faced with the problem of not having sufficient depth or ability in its purchasing groups and must therefore assign the responsibility to another function such as finance, data processing, systems, accounting, or materials management. The assignment of responsibility to an existing group within the corporate structure automatically defines the department head as the prime authority.

Another method of fixing responsibility is to establish a task force made up of representatives from several departments. In this instance, one individual should be selected as the group leader in order to provide proper guidance and decision in accordance with the objectives. The task force usually consists of representatives from purchasing, accounting, manufacturing, maintenance, and engineering. The product category should be considered when establishing the task force so that proper emphasis can be given to the ultimate user. For instance, a representative from the research department should be a member of a task force developing a contract on laboratory supplies and equipment.

There must be well-defined objectives so that management can evaluate the effectiveness of the program. These should include the following:

1. Improved service to the plant.
2. Reduced paperwork.
3. Reduced inventories.
4. Improved profits.
5. Regained floor space.

Specific dates should be established for the completion of the various phases of the program. These will include the following:

1. Selection of product category.
2. Vendor orientation.
3. Vendor proposals.
4. Vendor selection.
5. Price negotiation.
6. Materials survey.
7. Catalog of materials.
8. Plant seminar.
9. Inventory adjustment.

10. Implementation.
11. Review of performance.
12. Report to management.

It is difficult to fix any exact timing for each phase, but the first contract will probably require six to ten months to implement depending on the nature of the category.

CHOOSING THE PRODUCTS TO BE COVERED

The first few contracts should be confined to materials of a rather insignificant importance in relationship to the total plant operation. It is better to work out the bugs on a stationery contract than on a contract for bearings. Another category which is good to begin with is maintenance plumbing. The total dollar volume must be great enough to interest a vendor, and the transaction frequency must be relatively high. Some product categories which are applicable to Systems Contracts are as follows:

   1. Automotive supplies and repair parts.
   2. Bearings, pillow blocks, bushings.
   3. Electrical supplies.
 *4. Fasteners.
 *5. General hardware (hand tools, cutting tools, precision tools).
   6. Laboratory supplies and equipment.
 *7. Lubricants.
 *8. Lumber.
 *9. Maintenance and housekeeping supplies.
  10. Metals (steel, aluminum, bronze).
 *11. Office supplies and equipment.
  12. Paint and related supplies.
  13. Paper (fine and corrugated).
 *14. Plumbing and heating supplies.
  15. Printed materials (advertising, forms, boxes).
  16. Rubber materials (hose, belting).
  17. Safety supplies (gloves, goggles, glasses, shoes).
  18. Transmission equipment (gears, chains, pulleys, U-belts).
  19. Welding supplies.

Those categories marked with an asterisk in the above list are usually less critical in terms of product specifications and plant use and should be easiest to establish. Usually only a few days are required to determine the product category, and very often the decision is made when planning the vendor seminar. The product categories will undoubtedly indicate the suppliers who will be potential contract vendors. The number of categories considered during the initial attempts at Systems Contracts should be kept to a minimum.

VENDOR ORIENTATION

The objective of this phase of the program is to orient the prospective vendors in the basic concept and the responsibilities of a contract supplier to the requisitioner as well as to the company. When deciding which vendors to invite to an orientation, consideration should be given to:

1. Past associations.
2. Proximity.
3. Brands represented.
4. Inventory potential.
5. Financial responsibility.
6. Management ability.

These guidelines will also be helpful in determining how many vendors will be invited. There is no reason to invite a vendor who does not have the potential to service an account. It is better to have a meeting at a later date to explain to him why he was not considered rather than to let him go through the motions. In certain instances only one vendor may be considered, and this action must be explained not only in a logical manner but also in an ethical manner to other vendors. Successful vendor meetings can be held on either a group or an individual basis. As a first step, a letter of invitation should be directed to the top executive of the potential vendor explaining that there will be a meeting to outline a program designed to simplify and improve the future working relationships between the customer and the suppliers. A letter which has been used successfully and which outlines most of the objectives of the seminar is as follows:

Mr. (President, Sales Manager)
XYX Supply Company
Portland, Maine

Dear Sir:

The complexity of modern-day industry has meant that we must continually strive for improvement in order to remain profitable and successful in our field. As your customer, our success can influence your success.

During the next few months we anticipate a change in our procurement methods which may affect your working relationship with our company. We expect to simplify our order procedures by utilizing the Systems Contracts concept.

You have been selected as a potential supplier on the basis of a preliminary study and are requested to attend an orientation seminar on (specific date, time, and place).

Yours very truly,

This type of letter clearly states the objectives without getting involved in too much detail. Many vendors are aware of the existence of Systems Contracts but do not know specifically how they function.

The invitation should always be extended to top management of the vendor because we must make sure it fully understands just what the concept involves. A salesman might be interested in the meeting, but he is seldom in a position to make a definite commitment for the vendor he represents. The full impact of the concept will also become apparent to the vendor when he realizes that the contract is only extended to one vendor for the materials covered. This need not be stated in the invitation but should be made clear during the orientation.

The orientation seminar should be conducted by the person responsible for the implementation of the concept. In this manner, the vendor will know whom to contact for additional information.

The group meeting has been most successful as a means of making sure that all potential vendors receive the same information. This also puts their minds at ease because they know that all receive the same story at the same time. When conducting separate or individual vendor meetings, care must be taken that each one is told the same story within a reasonable period of time.

The importance of the seminar and the long-lasting effect it will have on the vendors demand that the meeting be informative and as complete as possible. The vendor must know the why of Systems Contracts as well as the how.

An excellent method of conducting a vendor seminar is to follow a step-by-step outline of the existing procurement method. This can be illustrated in flow-chart form showing the requisition point, store function, purchasing, and so on as was done in Exhibit 1.

Once the existing method has been defined, the Systems Contract concept can be outlined in the same manner so that a comparison between the two systems can be made. The reduction in paperwork and directness of the new method will be immediately apparent to all concerned. The advantages to the vendor should be stressed so that he does not feel that the concept is one-sided. These advantages will include the following:

1. Dependable business relationship.
2. Long-lasting agreement.
3. Work simplification.
4. Preferred source.
5. Improved profit.

A period of questions and answers should follow the formal part of the presentation so that the vendor will have an opportunity to clear up any doubts he might have concerning the program.

Each vendor should be furnished a list of specific items which represent a significant portion of the materials to be included in the agreement. Usually only those items of highest volume represent any significant dollar value. By confining the list to a small number of materials the vendor will be able to make a statistically accurate proposal without becoming involved in a tremendous amount of paperwork.

The vendor should be requested to return his proposal by a specific date. When two or more vendors are involved, a sealed bid is most preferred.

The question of price should be covered. When and how depends largely on the type of meeting. The fact that price is not a major determining factor but only a part of the total consideration should be brought out in the seminar. The exact basis of the price structure might better be discussed in private meeting. One more reason why purchasing people should have the prime responsibility of developing Systems Contracts is that they are professional negotiators.

Those vendors who are not invited to attend the orientation seminar will undoubtedly get wind of the fact that one was held and will begin to ask questions. They will become alarmed over the fact that they may lose business and can create problems with more frequent plant visits and letters. Rather than wait for this to happen, it is better to face facts and hold meetings for those vendors not considered a prime source of supply—usually on an individual basis because of the personal nature of the reasons given for why they were not considered. They can be given some hope, however, by the fact that the concept involved only the low-value items and the high-value materials will continue to be bought on a purchase order basis. Once these vendors have been told the criteria for selection and rejection, they usually accept the situation. Occasionally they will not accept the explanation and will try to go over the heads of those responsible for developing the concept. In this instance, top management must give its complete backing to the concept and the decisions made by the group. Again, by making top management aware of Systems Contracts and securing its agreement in the beginning, situations such as this can be overcome without difficulty.

THE VENDOR'S PROPOSAL

The proposal from the vendor should outline exactly what protection the vendor requires and what services he agrees to provide. These should include the following:
1. Amount of inventory.
2. Delivery schedule.
3. Emergency services.
4. Invoicing procedure.
5. Price protection.
6. Value analysis programs.
7. Identification of major and minor lines represented.
8. Termination requirement.

In addition, the price quotations based on the list of materials furnished at the vendor orientation seminar should be included with the proposal.

A simple form can be developed which will help standardize the proposals and will be most helpful in the vendor selection phase. Generally, about two to three weeks is sufficient for a vendor to prepare the proposal.

Formula pricing is an attempt to simplify the problem of pricing the vast number of materials covered under a Systems Contract. The formula used is C + FF = SP, or Cost + Fixed Fee = Selling Price. Under this method, the vendor uses his cost as the basis of his selling price. These costs are known to him and can be verified by the invoice he receives from his supplier (the manufacturer). The vendor negotiates a fee or gross profit with the company, and this fee is expressed in terms of a percentage. Thus if a specific item is invoiced by a manufacturer to a distributor at $1 each and his fee is 25 percent, the selling price to a Systems Contract customer will be $1.25 each. The $.25, therefore, represents the vendor's gross profit. Included in this margin will be the normal cost of doing business, such as sales expense, administrative expense, shipping expense, and advertising. This method is very easy to control in that the vendor can be called upon to substantiate his selling price by furnishing an invoice showing actual costs. Vendors, nationally, have indicated their complete agreement with this method of pricing, and even go so far as to allow bona fide personnel from their contract customers to audit their records.

There are several additional benefits associated with formula pricing. It frequently results in lower prices to the customer where the supplier takes advantage of quantity discounts. For example, a product which previously cost the distributor $1 each and sold for $1.25 (C + 25 percent = SP) now, as a result of a quantity discount, costs him $.90. The fixed fee percent remains the same, but his selling price to the customer is now $1.125 each. The cost reduction to the vendor is $.10, but the cost reduction to the customer is $.125. There might be some objection to the fact that the vendor is losing dollar profit per transaction; however, the total dollar volume will improve substantially and the total dollar profit increase accordingly.

Obviously, there are no set rules for determining what the fee should be, but it must represent a profit to the distributor. A customer would make a serious mistake in forcing a contract at a loss to a vendor because the vendor will not be able to provide the services required for a successful program. Ultimately the contract will either fail or a higher fee will have to be negotiated. Where a vendor is not able to adapt to the formula-price concept, normal price negotiation methods will be sufficient.

The vendor may establish a different fee for various categories of materials or for a specific item within a category. This will reflect more competitive prices where substantial volume is involved. The formula pricing method usually will not work successfully on contracts written with the prime manufacturer of materials. This is because few manufacturers will divulge their true costs. When a contract involves direct buying, it is best to accept a published price list and negotiate a discount or negotiate each price individually.

VENDOR SELECTION

The pre-selection process should indicate which vendors have the basic potential to function under a Systems Contract. The key to a successful contract is the proper selection of the source of supply. Many a purchasing agent has been completely fooled concerning a supplier's ability because of a dynamic personality on the part of the salesman who calls on him. In addition, other vendors with excellent capability may be overlooked because of personal likes or dislikes.

In order to insure that the vendor selected will be the best possible source of supply, an analytical approach is recommended. Assuming that the vendors were invited to submit a proposal, we must thoroughly evaluate the proposals and, in addition, conduct an intensive study of their organizations, which will greatly assist in the ultimate decision.

The responsibility of vendor selection should be assigned to an evaluation team made up of members of the purchasing department, the requisitioning area, and accounting so that proper emphasis can be given to each function. In order to help the evaluation team reach an objective decision on a prospective vendor, a vendor-evaluation report should be developed (see Exhibit 9 for a sample). Much of the information required is obtainable from outside sources, but an actual visit to the vendor's location will be required in order to complete the data. The vendor should be told that he will be visited by the evaluation team. The actual merchandise mechanics of the visit should be disclosed in order to prevent any last-minute window dressing on the part of the vendor, because it is imperative that the vendor evaluation represent a true picture of his operation.

In the report shown in Exhibit 9 you will note that there are 100 points attainable by a vendor, the points for each category varying in accordance with their importance. The team should score each vendor on an individual basis and then use the total score to help select the best supplier.

Occasionally, a vendor is reluctant to divulge certain information concerning his financial status or future plans, and these decisions should be respected. The points for these categories in all probability will not be too critical, but should a close situation between two vendors exist, they may have a bearing on the decision.

During the actual inspection of the vendor's premises, the team should ask specific questions concerning the information it is seeking. Evasive answers or other indications of poor judgment should be noted so the team can arrive at agreement on the vendor's rating.

Some things to look for when visiting a supplier that might indicate ability are the following:

1. Type of warehouse:
   a. Multifloor.
   b. Single floor.
   c. Wood.
   d. Brick.
2. Inventory control:
   a. Perpetual.
   b. Minimum/maximum.
3. Order flow:
   a. Receiving.
   b. Inventory picking.
   c. Shipping.
   d. Accounting.

VENDOR EVALUATION REPORT

	Actual Rating	Maximum Points for Each Category
1. Company name: Address City and state Telephone number Other locations	( )	5
2. Officers: a. President b. Sales manager c. Office manager d. Warehouse manager		
3. Type of company	( )	1
4. Major controlling interest	( )	1
5. Dun & Bradstreet report	( )	5
6. Major product lines represented:	( )	10
7. Approximate value of inventory	( )	5
8. Annual inventory turnover	( )	1
9. Number of employees: a. Sales b. Office c. Warehouse	( )	5
10. Financial statement	( )	5
11. Business history and future plans	( )	1
12. Management succession	( )	1
13. Past relationship: a. On-time delivery b. Price c. Quality d. Engineering ability	( )	10
14. Personal observations: a. Order processing b. Purchasing c. Invoicing d. Equipment e. Delivery/proximity f. Housekeeping g. Type of building(s) (fireproof, sprinkler systems)	( )	25
15. Systems contract concept: a. Existing contracts b. Implementation phase c. Interest d. Capability e. Price quotation	( )	25

EXHIBIT 9

    4. Expansion potential:
       a. Property.
       b. Cost.
       c. Desire.
    5. Sales and advertising programs.
    6. Union status of employees.

Other subtle indicators are also available, such as general company morale, attitudes, neatness, and efficiency.

Each of the above items may or may not be included in the evaluation checklist; however, the more complete the data, the more accurate will be the analysis.

It must be remembered that a Systems Contract is a long-term association, and anything which could cause delay in or hindrance to the smooth flow of business between the company and the vendor is a source of potential trouble.

The summary of the team's rating should be noted immediately after the vendor visit so that each representative's viewpoint will be fresh in his memory. A recap sheet can be made to represent the consensus of opinion for later comparison with the other vendors.

Once all of the vendors have been evaluated and the results reviewed, one vendor will probably stand out as the best possible supplier for the materials under consideration for a Systems Contract. In all probability, this supplier will have been recognized as the best source before the evaluation, but now there is an analytical verification of this opinion.

If more than one vendor is indicated, the team should then rely on its good judgment and make a decision. In some instances it is possible to split the contract between two good vendors in such a way as to give each one of them a profitable share of business. When this is done, it should always be accomplished in such a manner as to make each one responsible for specific categories and not have each one compete with the other on the same item.

Once the vendor has been selected, those vendors who were unsuccessful should be notified. This should always be done in person in order to allow them the opportunity to ask questions with regard to their failure to qualify. This is another case where the vendor selection report will be of great assistance. It will be able to pinpoint weaknesses and help the vendors become more aware of their problems. It can also be pointed out that the opportunity to participate as a supplier on those materials not covered by contracts still exists.

MATERIALS SURVEY

This survey should be made before the agreement is actually concluded with the selected vendors. The objective of the plant materials survey is to identify all of the high-volume repetitive materials to be supplied by the vendor under a Systems Contract. This phase is usually performed by the vendor to be contracted with and therefore should not be attempted until the vendor has been selected. The survey will provide the basis for the catalog of materials. The vendor salesman or other personnel familiar with the lines represented by the vendor will probably spend several days checking through the various files maintained by the company. This means that the customer must provide as much information as possible to the vendor. The problem of ethics is sometimes mentioned because the vendor is given information concerning his competitors. This may be true, but the competitors have been eliminated by this time and all of the information pertains to past history. Since no bid is involved, most purchasing agents agree that the access to basic information by the vendor to develop the catalog is within good ethical standards. If this poses a problem, the price information usually found in company records can be deleted without too much difficulty. The records most frequently used in the product survey include closed purchase orders, inventory control cards, traveling requisitions, and bills of materials. If there has been prior association, the vendor will also have a wealth of product knowledge available based on his past experience.

The materials determined by the vendor as potential catalog items can be noted on regular 3 x 5 index cards. The items should be described in accordance with the customer's nomenclature and should include the size; pack; brand; and annual, monthly, or weekly usage. One item per card is recommended; however, a range of similar materials is sometimes included on a single card in order to conserve time.

Many vendors make the mistake of trying to be a total source of supply to a customer. This leads to trouble on those items with which they are not familiar. It is better to concentrate at first on the strong lines represented and then proceed to secondary products at a later date. Once the confidence in both the system and the ability of the vendor has been firmly established, the possibility of taking on new product lines can be discussed.

When the items have been identified by the vendor, a preliminary meeting should be held with the people responsible for product specification. At this meeting, agreement must be reached concerning the acceptability of the brands furnished by the vendor if they are different from those currently in use. Very often, brand preferences have been established after many years of association, and management must recognize the necessity to accept comparable materials based on specification and performance. If the material cannot be reconciled because of some peculiarity, the item should not be considered a part of the contract. Replacement parts are a good example of materials which are difficult to substitute. On the other hand, many items are quite similar. National brands of light bulbs all fit the same socket and light up when the switch is turned on. The cost value of an individual bulb is too low to warrant verification of the various claims of the manufacturers. Final agreement as to acceptability of these materials by the plant will allow for the construction of the catalog. The time required to complete the materials survey will depend on the number of items involved and the acceptability of the specifications.

CATALOG OF MATERIALS

The catalog is a vital part of the order and invoicing process and must be prepared in a logical manner. It is basically an extension of the plant materials survey published in book form. The actual time required to complete this phase is usually six to eight weeks once the materials survey has been completed. Much of the time will be taken up in pricing the materials. The balance of the time is required for printing.

A catalog can be greatly simplified by using various colors of paper for the different categories represented—for example, red pages for plumbing and heating, blue for electrical, orange for general hardware, white for fasteners.

Another suggestion is to establish an index for each basic category where there is a major vendor involved. Fewer complete catalogs need to be printed if a department has a need for only a portion of the total book. There is no reason why an electrician would need a catalog containing laboratory supplies as he would seldom, if ever, have a requirement involving these commodities.

The front page of the catalog should include the name of the vendor and basic information such as mailing address, telephone numbers, and persons to contact during regular business hours. A listing of people and telephone numbers for emergency and after-hours contact should also be shown. The vendor must make sure that the emergency numbers will reach someone in authority at all times when this kind of service is required.

One way to help the requisitioner reduce errors in using the catalog is to include pictures of the materials described. This is quite simple to accomplish with today's methods of reproduction, and the added cost will be more than offset by the ease of implementation.

The total number of catalogs required will be determined by the number of users. Two types of catalogs are printed; one that is priced and one that is unpriced.

The priced catalog is issued to (1) the vendor, (2) accounting, (3) purchasing, and (4) auditing. These catalogs should be numbered and assigned to a department or individual to prevent their loss. Price information is considered confidential and should be treated as such. Occasionally, engineering or other departments require a priced catalog, but the decision to provide this information should depend on the actual need.

Unpriced catalogs are issued to the various requisitioning points throughout the company. As previously noted, it is very difficult to keep a check on which individuals are assigned unpriced books because of the number of people involved and normal personnel turnover. The books can be assigned to a department; and when changes to the catalog are made, the department head should be notified.

The cost of printing contract catalogs is very often split evenly between the vendor and customer, but some vendors underwrite the entire cost of the catalog in order to be able to use the same material for other customers.

DOCUMENTATION OF THE AGREEMENT

The name Systems Contracts implies that some type of document is used to formalize the understanding between the vendor and the customer. Certainly the delivery cycle, price basis, and invoicing procedure should be in writing to prevent any misunderstanding at a later date. Several methods are used to accomplish this: letter of agreement, purchase order, contract form. Care should be taken to prevent too much legalization of this area since the concept merely is a simple buy-sell agreement between a company and vendor.

Carborundum has developed an agreement which describes the essential points which might be included in a Systems Contract. It contains the following features:

1. Purpose of agreement.
2. Parties to the agreement and materials covered.
3. Terms.
4. Price schedule.
5. Renegotiation provision.
6. Price changes.
7. Audit of buyer-seller transactions.
8. Indemnification of seller.
9. Back orders; stock-outs.
10. Materials substitutions.
11. Delivery schedule for catalog and noncatalog materials.
12. Invoice procedure.
13. Termination.
14. Value analysis.
15. Contract changes.
16. Standard purchase order conditions and terms.
17. Assurance that terms and conditions of the agreement are made available by the supplier in the general marketplace.
18. Provision for sale of existing inventory to supplier.

Some of these features may or may not be required depending on the complexity of the contract involved and the total value of the transaction. A sample letter of agreement based on the above conditions is illustrated on the following pages. Perhaps the most significant reason for issuing a formal document, other than the fact that it is businesslike conduct, is that both parties expect the agreement to remain in force for several years and the agreement must continue to function in the event that the individuals who negotiated the original agreement are no longer connected with the program.

President
XYZ Company
Any Place

Dear Mr. ....

The purpose of this Letter of Agreement is to specify the terms and conditions of the agreement between The Carborundum Company (hereinafter referred to as the Contractee) and the XYZ Supply Co. (hereinafter referred to as the Contractor).

1. Contractee agrees to purchase and Contractor agrees to sell the *(basic category)* items covered by this agreement as listed in the *(category)* Systems Contract catalog developed for this agreement. Contractee also agrees to purchase and Contractor agrees to sell other noncatalog items not specifically covered by this agreement, using the Systems Contract order procedure. Deletions from, and amendments or additions to, this catalog may be accomplished by the written consent of both parties.

2. Contractee expects this agreement to become effective *(Date)* and to remain in force until *(Date)*. The terms of this agreement are specified in order to provide an opportunity for each party to evaluate its effectiveness. The specification of any expiration date should not be construed to indicate the intention of either party to terminate this agreement on said date. It is the express hope of both parties that this agreement will prove satisfactory and will be renewed on an annual basis.

3. It is agreed that items specifically covered by this agreement will be sold to the Contractee by the Contractor at the prices stated in the Systems Contract catalog developed for this contract and that these prices are considered net delivered Contractee's location as specified on the Material Requisition.

4. If Contractee's requirements change in a way to alter Contractor's costs, either party may in writing request the other for renegotiation of the contract prices. If no agreement can be reached, the contract may be terminated by either party upon 30 days' written notice to the other.

5. In the event of a general increase in the net invoice cost of one or

more of a manufacturer's product lines, Contractor may by written notice raise the price (these new prices will be effective the first day of the month following receipt of new contract catalog sheets). In no event shall such price exceed the list price of Contractor for such products.

6. In the event of a general decrease in the net invoice cost of one or more of a manufacturer's product lines, Contractor will by written notice to Contractee lower the prices (these new prices will be effective the first day of the month following receipt of new contract catalog sheets). In any case, the new prices shall become effective no later than 30 days after decrease in manufacturer's product lines unless agreement is obtained from the Contractee for a delay.

7. The Contractor agrees that the Contractee may at any time audit records of Contractor as necessary to determine that prices charged by Contractor are in accordance with the terms stated above, and that quantities and pricing as stated in invoices are correct.

8. Both parties agree to follow the procedure for order handling as specified in the Systems Contract Catalog developed for this Contract. Contractor agrees to have published and supply to Contractee both priced and unpriced catalogs to be used when ordering under this agreement. The cost of publishing these catalogs will be assumed by the Contractor.

9. Contractor will invoice Contractee and Contractee will pay Contractor on the 15th of the month and at month's end on the basis of tally sheets rendered for that period. These tally sheets are to be supported by a receipted original Material Requisition.

10. Contractor will stock an adequate supply of items for Contractee. Contractee will assist Contractor in forecasting usage, and Contractor will guarantee that there will be no stock-outs of cataloged items, unless due to circumstances beyond Contractor's control. Contractor will immediately advise requisitioning personnel of the Contractee when a stock-out situation occurs and delivery within the established time schedule cannot be accomplished. Contractor will take all possible action to provide these out-of-stock items with minimum delay. Contractee is free, however, under these circumstances to use any other source available to secure these out-of-stock items.

11. Contractor agrees to purchase and take possession of Contractee's stock on hand where this stock will, during the term of this agree-

ment, be supplied by Contractor. Contractor agrees to pay fair market value for items so acquired. The extent of such acquisition will be determined by the Contractee.

12. Contractee agrees to indemnify Contractor against any loss incurred as a direct result of obsolescence and discontinuance of any items carried exclusively and specifically for Contractee. This indemnification will not exceed three (3) months supply of any items which will be based on the last six (6) months usage averaged out. Contractor will do all possible to minimize Contractee's indemnification cost including the reduction of such cost by the sale of these items to prospective buyers for scrap or otherwise and by deducting the net value received through this sale from Contractee's indemnification cost.

13. Contractor guarantees that delivery of catalog items to the designated points set up by the Contractee will be made within twenty-four (24) hours after receipt of material requisition by Contractor. Seller will notify Buyer, by postcards addressed directly to the requisitioner, of delivery date of all noncatalog material.

14. No substitutions of material will be permitted on catalog items unless previously agreed to by the Contractee. In noncatalog items, the Contractor may deliver equivalent merchandise if requested items are not available when required but acceptance or rejection is the prerogative of the Contractee.

15. Contractor will do all possible to reduce Contractee's cost of material purchased through engineering studies. A target of cost savings of 2% of the annual sales dollar will be considered reasonable. The target, however, is not a necessary criteria to contract performance and will not be carried forth from year to year.

16. It is the responsibility of the Contractor that no representative of the Contractor will extend entertainment, gifts, gratuities, discounts, or special services, regardless of value, to any employee of the Contractee. Contractor has responsibility to report to the office of the Contract Coordinator any attempts by Contractee's employees to obtain such favors.

17. This agreement may be terminated by either party by not less than 30 days' prior written notice as a result of nonconformance. Cancellation may not be affected as a result of price renegotiation, except when initiated in accordance with Paragraph 4 above.

18. During the course of this agreement, all standard terms and conditions of the Contractor (copy of purchase order attached) and

not superseded by the preceding conditions particular to this agreement shall be considered in effect and are hereby incorporated as a part of this agreement.

19. Contractor represents to Contractee that the terms and conditions of sale described herein are also available to any other customers or buyers who may desire to contract with Contractor under such terms and conditions.

Please acknowledge receipt of this letter and acceptance of the terms and conditions contained herein by signing the enclosed copy and returning it to the undersigned.

Sincerely,

Accepted by ....   For:

Title ....

CHAPTER VI

Implementing a Systems Contract

Just before the actual implementation of the Systems Contract, a meeting should be held with all plant personnel who will be involved in the program. The purpose of this meeting is threefold.

1. Outlining objectives:
    a. Reduce paperwork.
    b. Improve service to plant.
    c. Reduce costs.
2. Discussing advantages:
    a. Requisitioner deals direct with vendor.
    b. Catalog of available materials.
    c. More items available immediately.
    d. Better control of departmental costs.
3. Explaining the system:
    a. Materials catalog.
    b. Requisition form.
    c. Approval points.
    d. Method of forwarding requisition to vendor.
    e. Vendor's responsibility.
    f. Receiving function.
    g. Requisitioner's responsibility.
    h. Accounting responsibility.
    i. Control measures.

The best person to conduct this seminar is the plant foreman or someone closely associated with the departmental or plant operation. This is now his program and should be treated as such.

Specific emphasis should be made concerning the requisitioner's responsibility to order only immediate needs. Reduced costs mean more profit and a more competitive selling price. These, in turn, mean increased business and more jobs in the long run. The requisitioners should be told about the control measures that are inherent in the system so that they will know that a system of checks and balances exists. This will help reduce the number of orders issued for private use and also help to cut down departmental inventories.

Vendor personnel should be encouraged to attend the meetings with the plant personnel so that the vendors can become better known and can answer any questions concerning the supplier's function. It is a good idea for the vendors to extend an invitation to the plant personnel to visit the vendors' warehouses in order to demonstrate how they control inventories. By seeing that materials are actually on the shelf, an excellent impression is made on the requisitioner.

A step-by-step order procedure should be provided for each person who attends the meeting. The order procedure should be included in the front portion of each catalog. The order procedure covers both cataloged and noncataloged materials. An example of an order procedure used by many companies follows. (Note that the order procedure for noncataloged items indicates that these materials must be ordered on a separate requisition and payment is based on a separate tally sheet. This method is used where the frequency of noncataloged requisitions is in excess of 20 percent of the total number of transactions or where the dollar commitment is significant.)

ORDER PROCEDURE

Standard Stock Items:
1. These items are those listed in the catalog. All orders are to be written on a three-part materials requisition.
   a. Each requisition will show the requisitioner's name, delivery point, charge number, and so on.
   b. Requisitions must be approved or written by one of the personnel

as indicated on the attached listing. In the event of an emergency, the supplier may issue a requisition with the approval of one of the authorized requisitioners.

    c. All three parts of the requisition will be forwarded to the supplier.

2. The supplier will assign a requisition number in sequence to each set of requisitions as received and stamp his name in the upper left-hand corner of each copy for identification.

3. Unit costs and extensions will be made by the supplier on the original and supplier's copy of the requisition (Copy No. 2). No prices will be indicated on the shipping copy of the requisition (Copy No. 3).

4. The original copy of the requisition will be returned with each order to the company receiving department. The receiving clerk will forward the original to the accounting department after signing his name verifying acceptance.

5. The third copy of the requisition will serve as the shipping paper and will accompany each order. Where more than one package is involved, the requisition number should be indicated on the package. The receiving clerk will visually check quantities received with the third copy of the requisition and forward to the requisitioner. The requisitioner will verify the items received. If the order is incomplete or the wrong item received, the requisitioner or receiving clerk will contact the vendor immediately.

6. The supplier will enter the total of each requisition on a two-part tally sheet using the requisition number for reference (sample attached).

7. The original of the tally sheet will be forwarded to the company accounts payable department concerned for payment every 15 days and/or no later than the first working day of the subsequent month.

8. The accounts payable department will verify the tally sheet with the signed original requisition and the confidential priced catalog.

Noncatalog Items:

1. These items are those ordered from the supplier but not listed in the standard catalog.

    a. All orders for noncatalog items are to be written on a separate three-part materials requisition and should not be included with standard cataloged items.

    b. Approval and distribution is as shown for standard items.

2. The prefix "NS" (for "nonstandard," or noncataloged) will be indicated for each requisition number assigned.

3. Extensions and distribution of copies will be the same as shown for standard items.

4. A separate tally sheet using the prefix "NS" in the upper left-hand corner will be used for noncataloged items.

5. Payment will be made immediately upon receipt of goods and the original copy of the noncataloged tally sheet.

INVENTORY ADJUSTMENT

After the materials category is determined, the company store inventory should be the subject of attention for major reductions. At the same time, the vendor should be in the process of increasing his inventory to prepare for the actual implementation of the contract. Regardless of how good his intentions are, there will undoubtedly be a sizable inventory left over in the company storeroom when the contract is ready for implementation. At this point, there are two ways of taking care of this situation.

One is to *work off* the inventory and order nonstore items from the vendor. This is not a very satisfactory method because some store items represent a six-month or longer inventory and the actual commitment to the system will be delayed indefinitely.

The second is to *sell back* the existing inventory to the contract vendor. This creates a clean cut-off situation and allows the system to begin on a specific date. Almost every vendor who has been approached has been agreeable to this condition, and it should be discussed during the negotiation stage. The supplier buys all of the materials regardless of brand or origin if they are items listed in the catalog. The price credited is the established Systems Contract price. Rather than actually pay cash for these materials, most vendors prefer to issue the customer credit which is applied to the first few months of operation. Where there is a significant quantity of materials involved, the company and the vendor should share the cost of transferring the stock. Additional protection should be given the vendor on brand items he does not normally stock so that, in the event these become obsolete at a later date, the company will bear the burden of expense of obsolescence. In order to keep the risk factor at a minimum for the vendor, those materials which in his opinion are obsolete should be eliminated from the transaction. The company should then decide on a method of disposal so that they can be physically removed from the storeroom. It is not enough to simply expense these items from an inventory account; the real cost is in their actual presence.

It is a good practice to delay sell-back for a few weeks during the implementation phase. Those materials covered by a Systems Contract which are destined for sell-back or disposal should be frozen in inventory in order to make the requisitioners dependent on the vendor as his source of supply. In the event of an emergency, the materials could be used. Once the system is functioning smoothly (about three to four weeks), the actual removal of materials can begin.

ACTUAL IMPLEMENTATION

At this point, the requisitioner will actually order his materials direct from the vendor under the Systems Contract. Obviously, this is a very critical time, and those persons responsible for proper implementation must be sure that all areas are ready. A checklist, which outlines the major function of each area, has been developed for this purpose:

1. Vendor-priced catalog completed:
   - Physical inventory corresponds with cataloged materials.
   - Order processing—incoming, accounting, shipping.
   - Blank requisition forms.
   - Inventory control minimums established.
   - Billing procedure established.
   - Emergency procedure.
2. Requisitioner—identified by department and name:
   - Materials catalogs issued.
   - Order procedure established.
   - Charge numbers assigned.
   - Approval points established.
   - Vendor contact known.
   - Noncataloged procedure explained.
   - Emergency procedure established.
3. Receiving—areas designated:

- Procedure established.
- Authority identified.
- Rejection procedure.
4. Accounting—procedure established:
- Control measures.
- Payment procedure established.
- Price-change procedure established.
- Noncataloged-materials procedure established.
5. Purchasing—approval of noncataloged price structure.
- Method of reporting to management established.

ESTABLISHING RESPONSIBILITY

The initial program to adopt Systems Contracts will probably be staffed by management people already swamped with responsibility. As confidence in Systems Contracts becomes more universal throughout the plant, the requisitioners themselves will begin to suggest new categories for contracting.

The expansion of the concept to its full potential will require that someone be assigned the responsibility of managing the entire Systems Contract program. Many companies refer to this person as a contract coordinator. He can be recruited from existing personnel whose workload will be affected by Systems Contracts. The individual must be capable of management as the responsibility of developing new contracts and reviewing existing agreements will require the following:

1. Interviewing vendors for potential Systems Contracts.
2. Analyzing vendor capabilities.
3. Establishing quotations.
4. Negotiating agreements.
5. Establishing logical in-plant procedures.
6. Reviewing vendor performance.
7. Analyzing reports.
8. Developing reports for management.

It is apparent from the above description of the areas involved that the contract coordinator should also have a strong purchasing background.

The contract coordinator, if such a position has been established, should be available to the plant during the first few days in order to provide assistance whenever needed. Where a team has been formed, each member might be located in certain key requisition areas. As the first day proceeds, the coordinators should visit the vendor to see how the orders are processed. At the time of receipt of the shipment, he should plan to be in the receiving department and check on the actual time of arrival against the time stipulated. Punctuality of delivery is important in order to establish routine. He should also follow the goods from the receiving department back to the requisitioner and make sure there is no delay in the in-plant delivery cycle. He should contact the accounting department after the verified original requisitions have been received there and check to see if any discrepancies are found. The next day or two, he should follow much the same procedure, correct all problems immediately, and be available for assistance for the next week but stay away from the plant. After two or three weeks, he should visit each area again and check to see if the system is performing as designed. Occasionally, one finds that a few people become overcautious and establish little personal inventories of materials. These should be discussed with the supervisor involved, and the practice discontinued. He should review the requisitions prior to payment to see how many errors have been discovered and notify the vendor to improve if this is a problem. He should, finally, check to see how many and what items are being ordered as noncataloged materials.

The number of problems that occur during the implementation phase and thereafter will usually be so few in number and so minor in nature that everyone involved will agree that the program can be considered operational after the first day. The term operational refers to the time when the system functions without the direct aid of those responsible for its conception.

REVIEW OF PERFORMANCE

The coordinator of Systems Contracts should review the program periodically in order to ascertain overall effectiveness. Experience has proved that an objective analysis on a regular basis keeps all parties to the agreement functioning in accordance with the objectives of the program.

Quarterly. He should review quarterly the closed file maintained by accounting. The original requisitions and corresponding vouchers should be checked for the following:

1. Proper signatures of requisitioner and approval point.
2. Quantities ordered, shipped, and received.
3. Order issuance-delivery time cycle.
4. Reorder frequency.
5. Pricing, extension, or other errors.
6. Number of noncataloged items requisitioned.

Occasionally there are requisitions which are filled by the vendor without the proper signature. This can occur as a result of a telephone order or simple error. If there is an indication that this is the rule rather than the exception, the people involved should be instructed to comply with the procedure. Employee turnover will also require that the list of approved signatures be updated periodically. It is advisable for a list of requisition approval signatures to be made available to the vendor, accounting, and purchasing; however, the company should not expect the vendor to police this list too closely. Accounting and purchasing should be the main control points. The vendor may be required to check approval signatures where the total requisition exceeds $100 or some significant amount of money.

Quantities requested can provide an accurate picture of how well the concept is functioning. If the requisitions call for small quantities of materials, it can be assumed that in-plant inventories are reduced to a minimum. This fact should also be verified by personally visiting the operating areas to check for any excess supplies. The number of "cross-offs" will indicate how well the vendor is meeting the plant's needs. Discrepancies in the amount shipped and amount received can indicate a problem with either the deliveryman or the shipping clerk, and these should be rectified immediately so that the plant receives all of its requirement on time. Breakage sometimes accounts for the difference in count and can indicate that perhaps an improved shipping container is required. Where theft is responsible, proper preventative measures should be taken.

Where the agreement was established, a specific order delivery cycle was prescribed. It was probably based on a 24-hour turn or perhaps longer if the material involved was of nominal importance. By checking the date issued with the date received, a good indication of the percentage of on-time shipments can be determined. A 98 percent effectiveness is considered excellent and 96 percent acceptable. Anything less than 95 percent indicates that some adjustment is needed. Most problems in this area stem from the fact that either the requsitioners order more than a normal quantity or the vendor is operating with too little inventory. Increased lead times on the part of manufacturers also can cause a vendor to experience some inventory control problems; however, this should not involve more than a few items at a given time and thus not affect his overall rating substantially. The number of emergency shipments required by the requisitioners should also be reviewed; and if this is a significant factor, an analysis of the transaction may indicate materials which should also be kept on the premises as well as in the vendor's inventory.

The number of reorder requisitions will be indicated by the requisition number. Whenever a "–1" or "–2" is added to this number, it indicates a partial shipment. If this is a frequent occurence, a meeting with the vendor is in order. This clearly indicates nonconformance and must be rectified as quickly as possible. Service is what the industrial distributor is selling, and this is what is expected.

Errors will occur wherever the human factor is involved, but they should have a tendency to balance out in the long run. If the errors always tend to be in the supplier's favor, there may be some question as to his ethical standing. Such a situation has never been uncovered to my knowledge, and this can be attributed to the proper conduct of the vendor evaluation. No vendor wants to risk the loss of a contract worth many thousands of dollars.

Those items ordered without a catalog number are classed as noncataloged. These orders are indicated by a prefix "NS" (nonstandard, or noncataloged) to the requisition number. A check of the items involved may indicate materials which should be added to the basic catalog in order to simplify the order process. This will also give some indication of the kinds of materials and the value of the noncataloged items ordered.

Annually. A personal visit to each supplier should be made at least once each year to inspect his operation. The information on the vendor evaluation report should be updated, and any significant changes noted. Actually, the buyer should view the inventory and determine how much is maintained for his needs. He should find out if other customers have adopted the same concept. He should determine if there are any changes that the vendor would like to suggest in order to improve the concept. These are a few of the matters which one might discuss. In addition, it is a good idea to inspect the true cost of a sample number of items, both major and nominal-use materials, to determine the vendor's buying bracket. If this is not possible under the terms of the agreement, a fair idea of the vendor's buying policy can be ascertained by the amount of material in inventory. An actual audit of a vendor's operation, even though part of the agreement, may in the long run prove more costly than the amount of money involved, and should be conducted only if there is a valid basis for this course of action. The value analysis effort of the vendor should be discussed at least once each year. As a prime source of supply, he should be in a position to make recommendations regarding product substitutions, new techniques, and so on, which can help reduce costs. Cost reduction efforts on the part of a contract supplier should be made a part of the agreement.

Biennially. Most companies feel that the agreement should be subject to competitive review every two years. The first year is usually devoted to stabilizing the program; however, the vendor should be in a position to defend his price structure and service after two years. Frankly, the actual termination of a Systems Contract because of a better price is rare. If it needs to be terminated, this indicates that either the original agreement was poorly negotiated or the vendor has not kept pace with the times and is therefore no longer competitive.

The procedure to follow should closely parallel the original method of vendor selection in that only a sample of the items covered should be used for the price quotations. A comparison of the bids will usually reveal that most of the competitive vendors will be very close to the present contract price. Depending on its total value, the contract should remain in force if the price differentials are less than 3 to 5 percent. For example, it would not be worth the trouble for a company to change vendors on a $50,000 agreement in order to save an additional $2,500.

On the other hand, a vendor occasionally quotes a price structure 8 to 10 percent below the current base. When this happens, the negotiator should have a serious discussion with the vendor to make sure he understands his obligations. Usually this situation occurs when a supplier is trying to break an existing agreement "at any cost." This type of vendor must be rejected because he cannot exist profitably over

EXHIBIT 10

the long pull and will, therefore, either require an additional margin or will be forced to discontinue the agreement at a later date. Again, sound business principles and intelligent management are the basis for Systems Contracts.

REPORTING METHODS

The fact that many areas, including top management, are involved throughout the planning, implementation, and operational stages of Systems Contracts requires that information regarding objectives, progress, and results be made available. Various reporting methods can be used, but these reports should be kept factual and concise. We must refrain from justifying an activity and remain objective. It has often been said that a picture is worth a thousand words: one of the best methods of presenting a factual report is to furnish photographs of the condition before and after. This technique is especially effective in dealing with inventory locations. A photograph of a company storeroom before Systems Contracts compared with a photograph of the same area showing machinery in operation speaks for itself. The photograph in Exhibit 10 was taken six months after the photograph shown in Exhibit 3. An office area now occupies the old office supply storeroom. The area has been turned from an expense operation into a profit center.

Progress reports showing reductions in the number of orders issued, invoices, materials, record keeping, personnel, and so on should be prepared and forwarded to key personnel at least once each quarter.

The monthly contract control report is a very simple report which can be obtained from one of several departments. The receiving department is generally responsible for this information although vendors sometimes provide the report. Essentially, the report consists of the number of requisitions, items ordered, and value of the transactions for a given month. An example of two months' reports can be found in Exhibits 11 and 12. These are two actual reports from Carborundum during October and November 1963. They provide an excellent illustration of the value of this type of control.

The left-hand column indicates the name of the contract supplier for a particular work area. It could be broken down further into specific charge numbers, but this is not required because of the small values

MONTHLY CONTRACT CONTROL REPORT I

MONTH: *October 1963*

SUP-PLIER	STANDARD			NONSTANDARD			TOTAL		
	No. of Reqs.	No. of Items	$ Value	No. of Reqs.	No. of Items	$ Value	No. of Reqs.	No. of Items	$ Value
A	424	717	13,630.76				424	717	13,630.76
B	41	63	1,658.02	16	20	378.96	57	83	2,036.98
C	84	133	2,429.70	71	109	6,107.63	155	242	8,537.33
D	139	479	2,853.90	110	159	1,841.09	249	638	4,694.99
E	60	228	1,244.31	91	173	4,029.09	151	401	5,273.40
F	43	69	2,374.42	51	75	1,710.85	94	144	4,085.27
G	21	31	1,154.69	3	4	14.06	24	35	1,168.75
H	40	59	764.22				40	59	764.22
TOTALS	852	1779	26,110.02	342	540	14,081.68	1194	2319	40,191.70

EXHIBIT 11

MONTHLY CONTRACT CONTROL REPORT II

MONTH: *November 1963*

SUP-PLIER	STANDARD			NONSTANDARD			TOTAL		
	No. of Reqs.	No. of Items	$ Value	No. of Reqs.	No. of Items	$ Value	No. of Reqs.	No. of Items	$ Value
A	381	732	12,228.13	—	—	—	381	732	12,228.13
B	55	80	1,444.86	15	19	395.39	70	99	1,840.25
C	84	183	2,289.51	54	91	1,064.27	138	274	3,353.78
D	188	654	3,308.78	89	190	1,641.79	277	844	4,950.57
E	98	277	1,375.04	92	162	2,334.38	190	439	3,709.42
F	39	66	1,428.51	50	81	1,094.81	89	147	2,523.32
G	20	35	818.47	—	—	—	20	35	818.47
H	41	51	553.09	—	—	—	41	51	553.09
TOTALS	906	2078	23,446.39	300	543	6,530.64	1206	2621	29,977.03

EXHIBIT 12

involved. The control by charge number is an accounting function and entered daily.

There are three major headings: standard—those requisitions pertaining to materials ordered from a contract catalog; nonstandard—those materials ordered from a supplier but not listed in a catalog; and a total of the standard and nonstandard requisitions.

There are three subheadings under each major column. The number of requisitions refers to the actual number of orders received in the plant from each vendor during the period. The number of line items and the value of the requisitions are also indicated.

The vendor's name indicates the basic category of materials—for example, Supplier *A* is the contract vendor on steel; so we know that in the month of October there were 424 requisitions placed and received for cataloged steel material. There were 717 individual items involved which cost $13,630.76 delivered net.

A comparison of several months' activity reveals many interesting facts. The grand totals indicate that in October there were 1,194 requisitions issued as compared with 1,206 in the month of November. This is statistically close and indicates a flat trend in activity. The number of items ordered is also very close—2,319 versus 2,621. The comparison of the dollar values of $40,191 and $29,977 indicates a significant deviation, and this calls for a more detailed analysis. Dollar volume of business with Suppliers *A* and *B* shows relatively little change in the months of October and November. Supplier *C* furnished the company with $8,537.33 worth of material in October and $3,353.78 worth in November. This is a major deviation and bears further study. We know further that the material involved was nonstandard in that this column shows $6,107.63 ordered in October against $1,064.27 in November. By checking through 71 requisitions obtainable from the file in accounting, it is possible to find out what materials were involved, who ordered them, who gave approval of the order, and everything about the transaction that might be of interest to persons responsible for plant operations, budgeting, and control of expenses. In this instance, the increase in expense was justified by the approval of the plant superintendent.

Since all of this information is available to the receiving clerk, it is a simple matter for him to keep a daily tally of the transactions and compile a monthly report.

CHAPTER VII

An Evaluation of Systems Contracts

Systems Contracts has been likened to a marriage between customer and vendor. The fact that both parties must want to work together is the binding force in Systems Contracts. The benefits from the association must be mutual; otherwise, the desire to continue the agreement would be lost.

HAS IT WORKED?

One of the major success stories of the Systems Contract program as developed at Carborundum is that the contracts originally negotiated there in 1961-1962 are still in effect today. Not only are they still functioning, but they are many times larger in dollar volume and materials coverage. All indications are that these same agreements will continue in effect for several years to come. Since the original agreements were signed, new agreements have been negotiated which have extended coverage of Systems Contract procedures to include virtually all MRO items. At the present time negotiations are under way to establish Systems Contracts on several high-volume production items.

Inventories have been drastically reduced. The central storeroom has been completely eliminated, and the area once occupied by this facility is now a major production machine shop. The reduction of inventories has even been noticeable down to the departmental substock level. This is a direct result of the ease of acquisition and the dependability of the suppliers. The individual requisitioner has discontinued building in a hedge on his requirement and now orders exact quantities to complete a given job.

Plant supervision expresses its complete satisfaction with the system by actively promoting new areas for coverage. Operating costs have been reduced through the elimination of several job classifications such as stock clerk, inventory control clerk, and expediter. The identification of thousands of materials available for immediate access has resulted in better job planning and more effective use of production time.

Shop supervisors also like Systems Contracts because it forces their people to plan ahead. The requisitioners can no longer blame someone else when they don't receive their supplies, and in the event of a slip-up they are only a few minutes away from a bigger and more complete inventory than was ever available under the previous method. The generation of more accurate job cost information through the use of individual charge numbers, coupled with direct-expense-as-received accounting charge numbers, has helped department heads keep an accurate fix on costs versus budgets. Exact quantity ordering has also created a better indication of true job costs.

Requisitioners have benefited through the direct association between themselves and the vendor. The knowledge of what is available has helped the requisitioner plan his work, and the availability of materials has allowed him to adhere to his work schedules. The vendor has assisted the requisitioner through the use of materials surveys, product substitution, and new techniques. Considerable cost reductions have been realized through the use of standard materials versus specials.

Accounting has simplified its method of handling invoices so that today 12 monthly or 24 semimonthly vouchers replace thousands of transactions previously required. Prices have become stabilized to a large extent through the policy of quarterly price revisions. The fact that freight and term discounts have been negotiated into the catalog price also improves the work flow in accounting.

Purchasing at Carborundum has also directly benefited from Systems Contracts. The amount of paperwork in this area has been reduced by an estimated 40,000 purchase orders annually. While this is a significant number, the additional paperwork normally associated with the issuance of a purchase order has also been reduced proportionately. It is estimated that at least five additional buyers and corresponding support personnel will be required to handle this volume of transactions. The orders that do go through purchasing today receive far greater attention than was previously possible. Routine sales calls are a thing of the past, and the improved sales effort on the part of vendor representatives has resulted in more productive use of the purchasing department's time. When a new idea is presented to a buyer at Carborundum, he has the time to give it proper evaluation. I might add that the buyers are also better trained today and are capable of understanding the more technical aspects associated with purchasing raw materials, capital equipment, and major expense items. Eighty percent of a buyer's time is now spent on that portion of procurement that represents 80 percent of the dollar commitment.

The Systems Contracts program has been a definite help in improving Carborundum's sales position from both a direct and indirect viewpoint. Systems Contracts has resulted in lower costs and, therefore, has allowed Carborundum to remain competitive and profitable. In addition, the concept has been used as a marketing device by the industrial distributors who represent Carborundum products to establish similar programs with their customers. As a result of this activity, Carborundum distributors have improved their sales volume, which in turn reflects a similar improvement in our sales volume.

Usually the materials involved in Systems Contracts are the low-value items which are seldom involved in trade relations activity. If they are involved, it is a simple matter to establish the same concept with almost any vendor. The main problem will usually be that of proximity. This can be largely offset by extending the lead time and delivery cycle to compensate. Where several vendors are involved, each one should be made responsible for a specific group of materials that is noncompetitive with the item responsibility of the other suppliers. Where it is not practical to set up a Systems Contract agreement, normal purchases of materials not covered by Systems Contracts are still significant and can be used in the regular manner to satisfy trade relations.

Systems Contracts are designed to handle *any* materials requirement. The main problem in negotiating Systems Contracts for certain materials is the lack of understanding, and hence willingness, necessary for both parties to cooperate.

Where a major production item is involved, the plant may not want to assume the full responsibility for order entry. Therefore, it may want purchasing to act as a buffer as well as a source of potential blame.

Vendors very often have a virtual monopoly on certain brands and can see no reason to change their present methods. The savings inherent in the concept for the vendor should often induce him to try the idea, but some vendors are difficult to convince.

Where several vendors are involved, and the order value is significant, it may be to the company's advantage to negotiate each order separately because of market fluctuations, total industry requirements, and so forth.

During the past several years, the author has had the opportunity to visit many corporations, large and small, and has found that most companies are attempting to develop programs similar to Systems Contracts. The methods used in Systems Contracting have proved most helpful in speeding up the time schedule because most of the bugs have been worked out of it at Carborundum. This is not to say that all companies can adopt the exact program without any tailoring (although several corporations have gone so far as to use our exact forms with only the company name changed), but the Systems Contract concept can be an effective method wherever repetitive materials are required.

Perhaps some objective comments from outside Carborundum would help the reader gain additional insight into the problems associated with implementing Systems Contracts at the plant level. The following remarks were made by Arch Downie, manager of capital purchases and plant services, American Cyanamid Corporation, Wayne, New Jersey:

> The Purchasing Department of any company is a profit center and as such must take the initiative in developing methods, techniques, and procedures to achieve the most favorable procurement of material to the overall net benefit of the company. For many years we have been attacking the problem of time and effort expended in the purchasing of store items—that is, MRO items of the low-cost, high-volume type. We tried many different methods, such as traveling requisitions, blanket

orders, and automatic release through EDP equipment; still we were not satisfied that we had arrived at the right solution. We were looking for an answer to the question, "How do we know we are buying best?" When we heard of Systems Contracting, it sounded as if a solution to our problem was attainable with a resultant contribution to our profit improvement program.

Our problems and reasons for seeking improved procedues for purchasing MRO supplies were the same as those of other corporations with a large number of plants to operate and a variety in types of production facilities. Our main problem, and one of the most difficult to correct, was habit. You might say habit was also the cause of some of the other problem areas such as obsolescence, inventories not in balance, too much paperwork, poor vendor relations, and high storeroom operating costs. We felt that if the systems contracting technique could solve some of these problems, we could then concentrate our manpower on more meaningful work.

Our first step was to learn all we could about Systems Contracting and its possible application at Cyanamid. We were impressed by what we learned and became more convinced that we had a solution to our problem. We then compared this method with other systems and procedures that might possibly be used in the purchase and handling of MRO supplies. Systems Contracting seemed to have more merit than any of the others, however, in that its procedures are simple, requiring no installation of sophisticated, costly equipment. Our final estimation of the potential savings indicated that this program should be actively pursued to derive the maximum benefit for the company. Purchasing management, convinced of the merits of Systems Contracting, took steps to obtain approval to program it on a companywide basis. The general manager of the Purchasing Division, in a presentation to corporate management, broadly outlined the program, emphasized management's desire to implement it, and established a long-range goal for savings that could accrue to the company.

Purchasing was on record, therefore, as desiring to improve stores-procurement procedures and thereby to contribute to profit improvement. Organizational adjustments were made in the corporate purchasing group so that proper emphasis could be placed on the Systems Contracts program. Consideration was given to what techniques might be used to present Systems Contracting most effectively to a multidivision, multiplant operation. It is evident that for the program to be effective it would have to be sold to the broad spectrum of personnel at all levels who in some manner were concerned with the managing, acquisition, handling, and financial aspects of MRO suppliers. A seminar method was chosen for plant personnel directly concerned with these materials on a more day-to-day basis. Because of the geography and the number of people involved, it was decided to hold these seminars at strategic locations.

We found most people reluctant to change habits to which they had become accustomed over the years. We had noticed that purchasing people in particular were not as well equipped to adapt to changes. This was not their fault. Too many men had been assigned to the purchasing function because there was no other place to put them. They were given the job but not the training necessary to perform well in purchasing. Therefore, they fell into the same routine as their predecessors and allowed the engineers and maintenance people not only to specify materials but actually to commit funds for them. It was in this type of operation that it was hardest to implement Systems Contracting because too many people were involved in the purchase of nickel and dime materials. We found that we obtained the best results by approaching the group as a whole and outlining all the advantages of the program for them.

Another problem we had was making the suppliers face the fact that they really had only service to sell. This was a time-consuming task and caused delays. But we knew that suppliers were a vital part of any plant system.

Prior to the introduction of Systems Contracts, the plants did not have an awareness of obsolescence. During the evaluation phase at the plant locations, however, everyone was made aware of this problem, and this fact encouraged the maintenance people and the storekeepers to go along with the program. Also, too little time was spent on evaluating how minimum and maximum inventory levels are determined, and little or no information was provided the suppliers concerning immediate or future plant requirements. Today the relationship between the plants and the suppliers has improved considerably.

As a result of Systems Contracts, we have found ways and means to cut costs throughout our plants, and even in our accounting functions. We are applying the principles of Systems Contracts to our spare-parts program and look forward to expanding this program to many other areas during the next five years.

Where Systems Contracts have been successfully implemented, those responsible for the program have adhered to the following outlook: the major theme of Systems Contracts is simplicity; the method of achievement is objectivity; the approach should be positive; and the agreement reached must be binding.

COMPARISON WITH OTHER PROCUREMENT METHODS

It is not the author's intent to discredit any system of procurement, but rather explain in detail how Systems Contracts functions and describe the benefits which can be realized by customer and vendor alike who adopt this method.

When evaluating an existing system, it is well to establish some basic criteria. These should include:

1. Description of present method:
   a. Forms required.
   b. Departments involved.
   c. Flow chart.
2. Type of vendors:
   a. Duplication of effort between company and vendor.
3. Record keeping:
   a. Degree of accuracy.
   b. Are they meaningful?
   c. Are they used?
4. Type of controls:
   a. Cost of controls.
   b. Value of materials controlled.
5. Plant service:
   a. Timing.
   b. Is it satisfactory?
6. Cost reductions:
   a. Prices.
   b. End costs.
7. Can present system be improved?
8. Advantages.
9. Disadvantages.

The survey of the purchase order system as outlined in this book will provide an excellent basis for a similar analysis of virtually any method. Some of the standard purchasing methods which can easily be compared with Systems Contracts are as follows.

1. *Quantity discount purchasing.* This method has a vital place in the total purchasing function; however, many companies fail to draw the line on where it is an advantage and where it becomes a disadvantage. Quantity purchasing involves economic order quantity (EOQ) buying and can be utilized to the best advantage when buying high-value materials such as manufactured parts, capital equipment, and raw materials. The money involved in this type of material is substantial enough to justify the expense of maintaining an inventory. On the other hand, when EOQ techniques are used to buy low-value repetitive materials, the cost of maintaining these items in inventory cannot be justified.

2. *Blanket orders.* In reality, Systems Contracts is based on the blanket-order technique. The difference is that only one vendor is responsible for the material under the agreement and the orders are placed directly with the vendor by the requisitioner. Most blanket-order systems eliminate a formal purchase order as such but duplicate the same procedure through the use of a blanket-order release. In many companies, there are even more steps involved when ordering materials on a blanket-order than with a standard purchase order. The main advantage of the blanket-order system is that it does pre-identify those vendors who can supply materials at predetermined prices.

3. *National contracts.* These agreements are very often excellent means of controlling standard specifications of materials used throughout a corporation. In addition, they often allow a company to pool the individual plant purchasing power in order to take advantage of a quantity price concession based on the total amount used throughout the corporation.

Agreements of this type are worthwhile only if they are enforceable. All too often, national agreements are little more than pieces of paper filed away and forgotten until it is time for renewal because the local plant can "buy better" and does. This method should only be adopted where it can provide the plants with better materials at prices below their ability to negotiate individually and with acceptable service to the users.

4. *Consigned inventory.* This is a very costly arrangement for the vendor in that he must duplicate the majority of his main inventory at the customer's plant. The material in inventory at the supplier's warehouse can be sold to many customers, but consigned stock at a customer's location is specifically for one plant. In addition, where more than one vendor is required, the problem of alloting floor space for each storeroom becomes far too costly to the customer. Other drawbacks such as favoritism, shrinkage, and auditing procedures contribute to the overall disadvantages of this method.

5. *Automatic reordering.* The use of computers and mechanical means of communication between customer and supplier is fast becoming a way of life. During the next few years major studies will be made in this area. For the present, Systems Contracts can lay a solid foundation for future automation because the majority of the basic needs of the plant are identified, standardized, priced, and available under a Systems Contract. The real problem facing an immediate changeover to an automated system is the capability of the vendor. Systems Contracts is a manual program which can be assimilated by all types of vendors. It is questionable if an industrial distributor can afford to install a costly computer system in view of normal sales volume and profit margins. During the next few years the costs of EDP systems will become more reasonable and should allow more suppliers to take advantage of these methods.

DATE DUE

GAYLORD			PRINTED IN U.S.A.